For the Love of Bees

For the Love of Bees
THE STORY OF BROTHER ADAM OF BUCKFAST ABBEY

Lesley Bill

NORTHERN BEE BOOKS

NORTHERN BEE BOOKS
© Lesley E. Bill

All rights reserved. No part of this publication may be reproduced, stored in a retrieval system or transmitted in any form or by any means, electronic, mechanical, photocopying or otherwise, without the prior consent of the copyright owner.

ISBN 978-1-904846-45-1

Printed 2009
Published by Northern Bee Books, Scout Bottom Farm, Mytholmroyd, Hebden Bridge, West Yorkshire, HX7 5JS.

Contents

Acknowledgements		vii
Foreword by Eva Crane OBE Phd (1912-2007)		ix
Author's Note		xiii
Chapter 1	Joining the Benedictines	1
Chapter 2	An Introduction to The Bees	7
Chapter 3	The Acarine Menace	13
Chapter 4	A new Broom In The Bee Department	19
Chapter 5	Planning Ahead For The Perfect Bee	33
Chapter 5	In Search	57
Chapter 7	The Road to the Middle East	63
Chapter 8	Onward to Asia Minor and Egypt	71
Chapter 9	The Buckfast Bee	77
Chapter 10	A Beekeeping Year at the Abbey	85
Chapter 11	Modern Methods	91
Chapter 12	Into The Eighties	97
Chapter 13	Brother Adam, The Final Chapter	103
	Bibliography	107
	Articles	107
	Books by Brother Adam	108
	Chronology	109

For the Love of Bees

Acknowledgements

My sincere thanks go to my former husband, Peter, for all the clerical work he put into the manuscript, to Mike Powell for his continued search for photographs and information and finally to Dom Leo Smith, the Abbot of Buckfast from 1976 to 1992, for his warm help and advice.

I shall always be grateful to Brother Adam for the questioning interest and deep enthusiasm he has awoken in me for bees and bee breeding, which has become manifest in practical application under his guidance.

For the Love of Bees

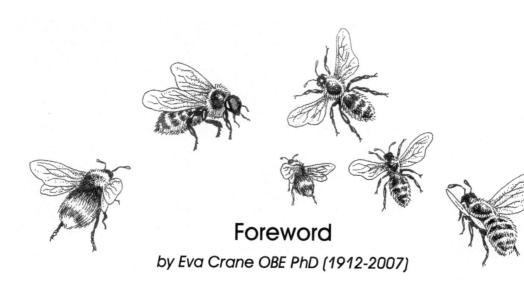

Foreword
by Eva Crane OBE PhD (1912-2007)

I have known Brother Adam for forty years, but this is not much more than half his life as beekeeper and bee breeder, which is the subject of Lesley Bill's biography. Beekeeping and bee research have been our common interests, and our links have been connected especially with his writings and their publication in English.

In January 1950 I became editor of *Bee World*, an international beekeeping journal which is published by the International Bee Research Association. Shortly afterwards I read an article by Brother Adam on his *Beekeeping At Buckfast Abbey* in Devon, published in the Swiss beekeeping journal Schwererische Bienenzeitung. I thought the article should be made available in English and, with Brother Adam's agreement, a translation was published in *Bee World* in December 1950. The article demonstrated Brother Adam's already long beekeeping experience, and also his willingness to reject established practices and theories where he was convinced of the need to do so. It started:

> 'Quite a few of our methods are not in line with principles generally accepted, or more correctly, they offended against rules acknowledged by most authorities on beekeeping - at least in England. In the course of the last thirty-five years we have established, and then adhered to, certain principles which are scientifically sound and also essential for good honey production - and the honey harvest is the ultimate aim in beekeeping.'

Beekeeping At Buckfast Abbey, a greatly enlarged text, was published as a book in German in 1969 and in English in 1975 and there were subsequent editions, both French and German.

Meanwhile, in March 1950, Brother Adam had set out on the first of his journeys through the homelands of different strains of honeybees. These journeys, which extended through Europe and beyond to North Africa and the Near and Middle East, continued for many years. His findings were reported in *Bee World* under the title 'In *Search of the Best Strains of Bees*', in 1951, 1954, 1961, 1964, 1965 and 1977, as well as in German journals. They were published in book form in German in 1966 and in English in 1968, and later editions - French, German, English and Swedish included additional material. The present book was finished just after Brother Adam had returned from yet another, more distant journey to Tanzania in Africa which has tropical races of honeybees of the same species as the European bee, *Apis mellifera*.

In 1954 and 1963 Brother Adam had written on bee breeding in German journals and in *Bee World*, setting out his own long experience and his deductions from it. The material was expanded as his experience became more extensive, and was published in German in 1982, and in English in 1987 as *Breeding the Honeybee*.

Brother Adam's steadfast dedication to beekeeping and bee breeding has thus included a programme of writing, first in German and then in English, on his three interlocking fields of interest, incorporating his new experiences and findings over four decades. He has also written widely in beekeeping journals on other subjects, such as making mead at which he is a great expert. The writings have made his work well known, and have won many adherents to his beekeeping methods. Buckfast queens have become much sought after, and a number of beekeepers have been attracted to make a pilgrimage to Buckfast Abbey.

Readers have been interested in Brother Adam's journeys through his accounts of them and in the bees and beekeeping of the countries concerned where he is warmly remembered. I myself travelled in some of these countries a decade or two later, and my companions were often those who had accompanied him. They seem to remember every detail of Brother Adam's adventures and interests, and I relived with them the excitements of his visit many years earlier.

As well as counting Brother Adam among my long-standing friends, we have a personal link through our names: mine by birth and his by conferment. This first became apparent to me in Mexico in 1957, when I visited Arthur Wulfrath who had built up the vast Miel Cadota enterprise - he asked me if there were any other beekeepers in England besides Adam and Eve.

Brother Adam has been a Vice-President of the International Bee Research Association since 1971 and I am glad to add my warm tribute to him, both personally and professionally, for his lifelong work for beekeeping.

Eva Crane
International Bee Research Association
Honorary Life President Director.
1949-1983

For the Love of Bees

Author's Note

It is now over seven years since I had my first meeting with Brother Adam which took place at his mating station on Dartmoor. The visit had been arranged some two years previously, but this is about the normal span of engagements for this world famous beekeeper as his calendar is always very full. It was with some trepidation that I stepped forward to acknowledge his warm greeting as I felt very much a novice even though I was already a keen amateur beekeeper running about two dozen stocks with my partner, Mike Powell. My fears were groundless, as although at first I found difficulty in understanding his soft broken English accent and lacked the courage to ask too many questions, his open enthusiasm for every aspect of queen rearing and breeding made each explanation an obvious pleasure to him.

I was content to watch the master at work and was greatly impressed by his ability to quickly open stocks and assess them with little apparent disturbance to the bees themselves. I was also struck by the enormous size and strength of his hands, still supple at the age, at that time, of eighty-two, though it was noticable that, under certain lighting conditions, his eyesight failed him. Being an ophthalmic optician by profession I sought to find out if any optical appliance would help and soon discovered that a combination of the eye disease, glaucoma, and complications subsequent to an operation for cataract was the root of the problem. Even so this does not deter Brother Adam from attending meetings, travelling at home or abroad or indeed just calling into a restaurant for lunch, which many folk ten years younger would not entertain.

At subsequent meetings the stories of his early years and how he came to be a monk at Buckfast when his home was in Southern Germany gradually unfolded. His memories of early beekeeping in England, the ravages of the Isle of Wight disease before World War I and his descriptions and first-hand assessments of some of the familiar names in English beekeeping such as Manley, Herrod-

Hempsall, and Snelgrove - many of whom were his contemporaries _ were both amusing and informative. Likewise were his impressions of some of the famous names abroad; the Nobel Prize winners Karl Von Frisch and Konrad Lorenz whom he had met at Vienna in the early fifties, to name but two.

His stories of yesteryear are fascinating. For example the main Plymouth-London trunk road was just a single dirt track in his early days in Devon and Adam can remember the Irish navies at the roadside breaking stone into chippings by hand, and being paid by the completed square yard. Or perhaps the fact that one of the Benedictine Fathers from Buckfast would walk every Sunday from the abbey to Princetown some 13 miles (20km) via the Abbot's Way. Even in the depths of winter after the morning office at 2.00 am, the dark figure would leave in the dark to cross the windswept boggy lands of Dartmoor in order to take the 8 o'clock mass at the local church before walking the 4-hour journey back to the abbey in time for lunch.

It is amusing too, to imagine the scene in those early years as Brother Columban took the bees to the high moor in wheel-barrows, with one brother on the handles and two more harnessed by rope pulling from the front, up hill and down over rugged countryside for mile upon mile. Adam also tells the tale of when he and two of the Brothers walked to the mating station at Sherberton and back in the snow as there were 10ft(3m) drifts around the abbey and they feared for the safety of the bees. Even by pony and trap, which was their normal mode of transport in the early days, the journey to Sherberton from the abbey normally took two hours as the occupants would have to get out of the trap and walk up the hills and again to go down any steep slopes. Anyone who has travelled the road between the two will know there is precious little flat ground anywhere. Once they had arrived at the apiary and off-loaded, the mare would be stabled over the hill at Sherberton Farm because, even though the adjacent field would be much more convenient, the headstrong mare was only borrowed for such occasions and had never been fully broken in and Adam knew full well he would never catch her again for the return journey. Such tales of transport we find hard to imagine in this age of the car and aeroplane, but these are all actual memories from over seventy years ago that make Adam and his listeners chuckle.

We also heard some amusing and exciting tales of his explorations in search of the various attributes of different races of honeybee. Starting in the comparatively civilised areas of Europe, these travels had taken him on to isolated Mediterranean Islands, the inhospitable lands of Asia Minor and North Africa and then finally South of the Sahara to the foothills of Mount Kilimanjaro. I found it all so interesting that over the months on my many trips with him, either to the eye specialist in London, to and from Heathrow Airport or on other sundry excursions we would ask questions and make notes in order to retain these fascinating stories. It was in this way that the idea of a biography evolved and when once the thought had been established, the research into the history of the Benedictine Order and the investigation into the immense undertaking by one man to reorganise and build a commercial beekeeping enterprise entirely on his own became a compelling task .

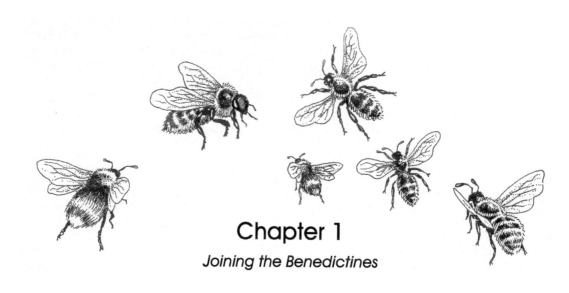

Chapter 1
Joining the Benedictines

'The eighteenth of March' the engine clattered as it thundered into the night. 'Nineteen hundred and ten' the carriages echoed as they rattled across the rails. A rather dishevelled small boy pulled up the edge of the blind and stared out into the blackness. The strange smell of the cinders and steam that permeated every part of the carriage was familiar now to the group of six youngsters who had been travelling by train for two whole days. They had come from Ulm in the south of Germany and after travelling the whole length of the country to the Hook of Holland a steamship crossing had brought them to London. There they had taken a horse-drawn taxi to Paddington Station for the final part of their journey to the Westcountry and the small village of Buckfastleigh in Devonshire.

Karl, as Adam was named then, was only eleven years old, and had mused aimlessly on that never ending journey through the strange countryside and even now was drifting back to his home in Germany. His brother Anton, some eight years older than himself, was away completing his military service but his father would be home from work and his eight year-old brother Friedrich would be playing whilst his sister Amelia and his mother busied themselves in the kitchen preparing the evening meal. He remembered the smell of fresh bread in the chill early morning as it wafted across from the little brick bakehouse with its red tiled roof. It was a good place, warm, friendly and inviting.

When he was born on 3 August 1898 in the village of Mittel Biberach, the Kehrle family owned the village flour mill, which sadly is no longer standing, and also worked some of the surrounding farmland. In later years Karl's father, who was a most enterprising individual, started a real estate agency and this necessitated the move into the nearby town of Biberach which lies midway between Ulm and Friedrichshafen. This whole district of southern Germany had been known as Schwabische since Napoleonic times and the old word is still used with pride in this area of Baden-Württemburg. Although the town was predominantly Catholic, the Protestants had been favoured by the Swedish during the Thirty Years' War and had been given the right to use the Catholic church. Even today this right still remains.

The church stood in the centre of the town and nearby was the schoolhouse, which was only a short distance from Karl's home. He liked school and was always near the top of the class but equally enjoyed playing with the other boys especially when they had the chance to swim in the River Reiss which meandered through the meadows on the eastern side of the town. The walk there took them past the local wax chandler's shop. An old stone step lead down into the dark interior where candles of all shapes and sizes were stored. The aroma of molten wax permeated the whole building whilst outside, during the long hot summers, flakes of beeswax would be spread on trestle tables and then left to bleach in the scorching sun. Herr Kehrle had often talked about keeping honeybees but much to young Karl's disappointment this had never materialised. He had observed the mysterious beehouses on a nearby farm and often wondered about them. Such houses still exist in the village today where the bees can be seen flying to and from the hives within the timbered buildings.

As the train journey progressed he remembered that Monday morning some weeks before when his mother had told him of her meeting with Father Mellitus, a monk from Buckfast Abbey in Devon. She was a deeply religious woman and the question she had put to her son was a simple one: 'Would you like to travel to England and join the monks at Buckfast and help them build a great abbey in praise of God?' He did not have to think long about his answer as he had always found the history of monasticism a fascinating study at school and believed these communities to be important centres of learning, agriculture and other skills. His answer was an equally simple 'Yes' and so the die was cast. Within a week or two Father Mellitus had written to Buckfast and Karl had received his acceptance. The next week he did not attend school but spent his time at home preparing for the journey. He knew little of what was in store for him but felt he had an ally in his cousin Ignatius from the next village who, some five years earlier, had done precisely the same as Karl was doing now and had joined the monks at Buckfast. The family had often spoken of this new life at the abbey but details from England were scant and in the way of small boys even his cousin's face seemed hard to remember.

The boy was dragged abruptly from his thoughts of home as the train jolted to a halt in a cloud of white steam. Doors banged, hobnailed boots clattered on the granite of the platform and a strange foreign voice rich with the burr of the Westcountry announced 'Buckfastleigh, Buckfastleigh' into the night air. The weary bunch of children in a strange land struggled with their luggage towards a new and rigorous way of life. Although Karl did not know it then, it would be thirteen years before he would be able to see either his family or his native land again.

For the next few years Karl would serve as one of twenty-four pupils in the alumnate. Each would be given a new name chosen by the Abbot and Karl was to be called Louis for this period. Unlike the preparatory school run by Buckfast Abbey today the pupils of the alumnate were all destined to become members of the community unless at some stage they decided to opt out and return home. The regime, used to ascertain the qualities of the boys, was a demanding one, always working towards acceptance as a novice. Some of the boys would be suitable for the priesthood but many would follow one of a number of crafts that were essential for the running of the abbey. Building, masonry, beekeeping, carpentry, cooking and farming were tasks all carried out by the brothers themselves in these early days, as there was no money available for the employment of outside workers.

The community into which the boys had now arrived had originated in France sixty years earlier with a monastery at La Pierre-qui-Vire founded by Pierre Muard. He had served his novitiate as a Trappist monk, a breakaway group from the Cistercians. The Trappists had returned to the ideology of the eleventh century when all luxuries were swept away and life was spartan in the extreme. In 1880 this order had been forced to leave France under the penal laws of the Third Republic. Finally, in October 1882, the group consisting of 12 Frenchmen, 3 Germans and a Scotsman bought the remains of the Benedictine abbey at Buckfast in Devon. The abbey had been founded in 1018 but had fallen into disuse and eventual decay following the dissolution of the monasteries by Thomas Cromwell, chief minister of Henry VIII, in 1539. All that was left of the original church and attached buildings was the remains of the abbot's tower which dated back to the fifteenth century and the stone from the ruins which had been incorporated into a private mansion. The rest of the monastery had completely disappeared.

The task of building up the community was not easy and when after a few years France relaxed her religious laws and some of the monks returned to their native land, the community became even more depleted in numbers. It was for this reason that one of the German monks, Father Mellitus Hauler, had on several occasions returned to his homeland of Schwabische in order to search for potential entrants to the community. It was not uncommon in this area for children to leave home at an early age and in some of the poorer regions they might even be sent to a rural family as a farm labourer to gain the relief of having one less hungry mouth to feed. Recruiting in France was not possible due to the youth of that country being involved in military service, so such campaigns were carried on in this area of southern Germany until the outbreak of war in 1914.

The Benedictine Order of Black Monks (so called because of the colour of their habits) that young Karl was to join was one of the strictest in Britain at that time. The choir monks, those who were to be ordained, spent seven or eight hours in the church each day. Starting at 2am they would rise for Matins, to be followed by Lauds at 6am. Mass was celebrated at 9 o'clock followed by None before lunch. Vespers was said at 2.30pm and Compline before retiring to bed at 8pm.

As a boy Karl, now named Louis, had only to observe these services on feast days and his mornings were spent in school, which included learning English, French and Latin. The afternoons were spent in recreation either on the playing field or playing cards or chess. The community also emphasized silence so that a sign language had been developed, but again the boys did not have to observe this rule until they had entered the novitiate. They were however only permitted to speak English or French, their native tongue, German, being forbidden after an initial period of six weeks. Meals were taken with the monks in the refectory and the food was plentiful but very plain. On one occasion each week the boys were permitted to eat meat. They also assisted at meal times helping as servers and with the cleaning of the hall. Life for the boys was not always subdued and, despite the hallowed surroundings, boys will be boys. Some seventy years after the event Adam still chuckles at the thought of one of his counterparts being tricked into sitting in a plate of custard!

Even in those early days the boy Louis who was to become brother Adam showed a love for nature. One of the boys had managed to catch a young wild rabbit and Louis kept it without difficulty in the greenhouse for some weeks. With some money his brother Anton had sent him he decided to buy a couple of other breeds, an Angora and a Belgian Giant, together with some oats on which to feed them all. They interbred quite successfully and after twelve months they numbered more than a dozen. Occasionally, as their numbers inevitably became excessive, one or two of them would be butchered for the meat that the boys were allowed to eat each week, but otherwise, Louis kept them as pets. One morning Father Mellitus called out in his usual friendly manner, "We need someone like you to look after the bees". Perhaps they did!

The great driving force in the community, at that time particularly, was the abbot. In those days the abbot's role was an exalted one and all would kneel before speaking to him. He was all powerful within the abbey having been elected for life and guided the monastery in the way that he thought fit. Buckfast was extremely fortunate in having in Abbot Anscar a man of exceptional talents. He served in this capacity from 1906 until his death in 1938. A brilliant scholar and theologian this quiet but tenacious man attempted to combine the simple spartan working life of the Trappist with both, the theology and prayer of the Benedictine and the compassion and awareness of the outside world of the missionary. He had spent some years in Rome studying with other priests from all over the world, and this broadened his outlook and was the catalyst that brought about the gradual relaxation of some of the more rigorous rules and regulations. Some of the minor changes such as the introduction of aluminium cutlery as opposed to the wooden forks and spoons that had formerly been used, caused some degree of comment amongst the brothers. On a far larger scale though it was he who, with just £5 in the offertory box, decided to start the rebuilding of the abbey church only a few weeks after his election as abbot. He set out to raise the money required but his faith was such that work started almost immediately and the first stone of the new abbey was laid in January 1907.

The Bath stone to be used in the work was brought from Somerset by train to Buckfastleigh and thence to the site by waggon and horses. These huge slabs were moved on rollers but the unloading of them was a hazardous task and one the young boys would watch from a distance. The stone then had to be hand sawn and finally dressed before being moved into position. Louis too helped with the dressing of the stone under the watchful eye of Brother Peter, the mason, who required the utmost precision from his assistants. The skills of these craftsmen and the disciplines they exerted upon the boys have served them in good stead over the years. To this day the older monks, and Adam in particular, show a desire for perfection and an eye for detail that one does not found readily in the modern world. Even now, over half a century later, Adam's work with his bees uses carefully thought-out routines showing that the training of his early instructors lives on.

Work on the rebuilding progressed slowly during the war years but a further injection of funds in 1921 enabled the stone to be purchased already dressed. This speeded up the project so that the abbey was eventually consecrated in 1932. This however is running ahead of our narrative because we find Louis leaving the alumnate and becoming a novice in 1914. Canon law decreed that the novitiate should last a minimum of twelve months. The first vows were then taken and after a further period of three years the final profession was made. It was not possible however to take the triennial vows until the novice had attained the age of twenty-one. Adam therefore would not be eligible until 3 August 1919, and thus he took his final vows in 1922. Thus the year 1916 saw him take his first vows and receive his new name, Adam, in remembrance of Father Adam Hamilton, the Scottish monk who had arrived with the others in 1882, having transferred from Ramsgate Abbey to act as interpreter for the French monks, none of whom could speak English. Young Adam was now able to wear the full habit of the order of St Benedict and became a recognised member of the community. As such not only were his religious commitments more exacting but he was also required to put in a full day's work except on Sundays and feast days. He had been chosen to assist the stonemason in the hard physical work of cutting and dressing the blocks and for two years he worked assiduously alongside Brother Peter, labouring on the great abbey itself.

Chapter 2
An Introduction to The Bees

Adam had not enjoyed good health since his arrival in Britain. For several months he had been homesick and with the rigours of the novitiate and the hard labour of the stone dressing he had become very weak. It was therefore decided in the spring of 1915 that he should help Brother Columban with the bees, which would afford him a little more sunshine and less strenuous work.

Brother Columban, a man of about sixty at that time, had been introduced to honeybees by his uncle when he was a youth. The severe winters in Southern Germany had forced them to keep the skeps, twenty in all, covered in carpet in a loft for some three or four months. In an article in the *British Bee Journal* of 1906 he says 'This made a deep impression on my young mind and filled me with admiration for the little labourers over whom so much loving care was taken'.

In 1895 he took over responsibility for the bees which had been part of the monastic scene since medieval times. Although the abbey had been founded in 1018, the original work was not completed for some two hundred years; incorporated into the ancient walls within the enclosure were a number of bee boles, three of which can still be seen to this day.

When Brother Columban took over, the eight colonies established by the new community had perished and had been replaced by driven bees. In the days before the movable-frame hive was in common use in England, honeybees were still kept in straw skeps. The wild comb within the skep 'was actually drawn from its sides and in order to remove the honey the combs had to be cut from the straw. It was much easier to do this if the bees had been driven from the combs. This was achieved by placing a second skep on top of the first, fixing them firmly together mouth to mouth with irons, and then with either fumigants or by drumming loudly on the sides of the lower skep, the

CHRISTMAS GREETINGS.

Among many Christmas cards, etc., gratefully received from time to time, as seasonable tokens of goodwill, by the Editors, the one illustrated on this page, to use a common colloquialism, literally "takes the cake." It was made by our esteemed correspondent, Br. Colomban, whose name will be familiar to readers by his recipe for making bee-candy, which proves his skill as a confectioner.

The cake shown in photo is made entirely of honey gingerbread—extensively used in Germany by all classes of the community—and is decorated with the sugar-piping used by confectioners. On the hive-roof being raised some time after its receipt, the "body-box" was found (much to the surprise of the recipient) packed full—from floor-board to roof—of honey-cakes and honey-sweetmeats, all of excellent quality and flavour, as attested by the many consumers who shared in partaking of the first "W.B.C." hive ever cut up and eaten!—[The JUNIOR EDITOR.]

'A unique Christmas Cake' made by Brother Columban appeared in the December 1905 issue of the *British Bee Journal*

bees would be driven upwards and cluster in the empty upper one. Such driven bees could be purchased quite cheaply but as it was often late in the season the colonies inevitably went into the winter in poor condition. Despite these problems, however, Brother Columban produced a surplus of honey in excess of 400lb (181kg) in his first full year.

Honey was an important product both as a household sweetener and for medicinal usage. Also the pure beeswax was essential for the abbey candles. These facts, coupled with an infectious enthusiasm, persuaded the procurator in 1900 to allow Brother Columban to obtain the *British Bee Journal* and other related publications, and to become a member of the Devon Beekeepers' Association. The increased knowledge of modern methods gained by study enabled him to make a start in reorganising the beekeeping activities. The huge double-walled hives in use at this time were mainly of French origin and of all shapes and sizes. Some of the hives held as many as eighteen frames and Columban attempted to house a nucleus at one end of each colony separated only by a ventilated dummy or dividing board, having individual entrances but using a common super. This proved unsatisfactory and led him to make special nucleus boxes, each divided into four parts containing three to four frames with a feeder below. He was able to winter these nuclei successfully and excess brood was used to boost the honey producing colonies.

At the time Adam joined Brother Columban there were forty-five colonies divided between two home apiaries; one where the cemetery is now situated and a second in an orchard which stood in front of the buildings now housing the cellars and great vats of Buckfast Tonic Wine. All the hives contained British Beekeepers Association Standard frames but the fabric quilts that were in common use throughout the country at that time were replaced by wooden slats, 3in (7.5cm) wide, nailed to small laths. These were found to give better ventilation than the quilts when placed directly on top of the brood chamber and were not propolised so much by the bees.

The value of good-quality young queens and their different characteristics was impressed upon young Adam and an article published as early as 1906 in the *British Bee Journal* by Brother Columban praises the Carniolan strain. Italian, Carniolan and White Star queens (Cyprian X Carniolan produced by Samuel Simmins of Heathfield, Sussex) all featured in the abbey apiaries. There is a record too, in this same year, of a Mr Abbot, the headmaster of the local primary school, obtaining 160lb (73kg) of honey from a colony headed by a Carniolan X British Black queen obtained from the abbey.

Brother Columban was also an outstanding pastry chef and with his experience as a journeyman cook in the Rhineland before he joined Buckfast it was only natural that he should also be in charge of the kitchens. Adam too had to help with this work and often in summer was left to prepare the evening meal whilst Brother Columban finished his work with the bees.

Even in later years Adam would creep out during the sermon on a Sunday morning to baste the roast for lunch. In the winter he was excused kitchen duties and was left to repair hives, make up frames and wire foundation. Every free moment he would spend perusing the American Journal *Gleanings* or the copies of the *British Bee Journal* that Brother Columban had stored with care, following with particular interest the sudden explosion of commercial beekeeping in North America.

At last Adam was happy. Life now had a purpose, a challenge. He enjoyed working with the bees immensely, but more than that, he was totally absorbed in the work both practically and theoretically. The drudge of work became a pleasure; the hours of solitude were no longer enough. He wanted to read, plan and try out all the new ideas he had studied.

With the onset of war in 1914, however, there came a time of tension throughout the country and, as many members of the community were of German origin, all were interned in the precincts of the abbey. Local opinion was still somewhat hostile and a ruling by the abbey that no photographs were to be taken there on a Sunday triggered a rumour that in turn led to a report to the Home Office that an underground tunnel from Buckfast was in direct contact with enemy V-boats (although the nearest coastline is almost twenty miles (32km) away). There was a top level investigation! Two furtive looking gentlemen from the Ministry, wearing the obligatory dark raincoat and trilby hat, called on Abbot Anscar. Tension mounted; the local people wanted action. The situation was finally diffused when most of the community followed the lead of the abbot and opted to become naturalised British citizens.

The national shortage of food supplies, due to the losses of merchant shipping, led to pressure being put upon all those not called up for the forces to work either on the land in food production or in other reserved occupations. This applied also to the monks and so the decision was taken to substantially increase the beekeeping activities of the abbey. This was duly done, the number of stocks rose from 45 to 100 and a 5 ton (tonne) honey surplus in 1917 satisfied officialdom and no further problems arose. The opportunity was also taken to effect some form of standardisation in the variety of double-walled hives in use. The model that predominated was the Burgess Perfection WBC hive manufactured in nearby Exeter. It was decided that all the other hives should be sold and the entire stock of Perfection held by the local firm should be acquired, making this the forerunner of the much larger commercial approach that was to come.

"BURGESS' PERFECTION W.B.C." HIVE.

The outer cases of this hive are square. This pattern of W.B.C. hive, i.e., a hive having outer cases to protect the brood chamber and supers, was introduced by ourselves, and was awarded the 1st prize (a bronze medal) at the NATIONAL HONEY SHOW, 1935, as the BEST HIVE for general use. The great advantages are, no outside plinths or fillets allowing rain to soak in and rot the wood; also, each lift when inverted will telescope down over the bottom outer case, thus reducing height of hive during winter storms, also giving the extra protection or warmth of three thicknesses of wood.

The hive consists of an improved floor having a deep entrance giving ample ventilation in hot weather, thus reducing the desire to swarm. A shutter with copper slides attached is used in cool weather (and during winter) to reduce height of entrance to 3/8 of an inch. The three outer cases are high enough to accommodate a brood chamber and three supers, and extra lifts or outer cases can be supplied to continue the height indefinitely. A roof having the wood top covered with zinc or galvanized iron unattached in any way to allow for expansion and contraction, makes it practically indestructible and also much cooler than when covered with painted canvas or calico.

The interior fittings supplied consists of our best quality brood chamber containing ten improved standard size frames with W.B.C. tin ends resting upon strong tin runners.

Price as specified, **48/6.**

If a detachable Porch is required	**1/6** extra
Insulated floor with four inches of cork chips	**3/6** extra
Extra taper Lifts 10 inches high	**7/6**
Wiring and fixing full sheets of comb foundation to the ten frames	**6/6**
Painting with three coats of "Ideal" special paint	**7/6**
Coating the outer lifts inside and outside with Rot Proof **Cuprinol**	**3/6**
Glass "Quilts"	**4/6**
Extra Thick Hair Quilts	**1/6**

An advertisement for the 'Burgess Perfection WBC Hive' as shown in their pre-war catalogue

Chapter 3
The Acarine Menace

At the turn of the century and even up to the start of World War I most cottagers in rural England kept a hive or skep of bees in one corner of the garden. One has only to read some of the novels by Thomas Hardy of this period to realise how wide this practice was and how important the products of the honeybee were to the country folk, many of whom had not seen the arrival of imported sugar or modern medicines. A disease that would decimate the honeybee in every corner of the land would obviously create quite a stir, and it did.

Some explanation of the background of this disastrous epidemic known at the time as Isle of Wight disease, which swept through England destroying an estimated 90 per cent of the bee population, may help to convey not only its severity and its impact on beekeeping in the country as a whole, but also the effect it was to have upon the direction *Beekeeping At Buckfast Abbey* was to follow. Much of Brother Adam's personal endeavours in years to come were influenced by the events of this troubled time.

There had been periods of unexplained losses of bees recorded since the-eighteenth century, and more specific instances of a similar nature in Derbyshire, Cornwall and other parts of the country at the beginning of the twentieth. Suddenly, late in the year 1904, reports started coming in from the Isle of Wight of severe colony losses in the south-east corner of the island. The problem spread quickly and complaints of dead and dying bees presenting malformed wings, inability to fly, crawling and gathering to clusters in the grass soon flooded in from all over the island. Despite efforts to seal off the island the disease, described in the national newspapers of the time as a 'terror inspiring epidemic', finally reached the mainland in 1908.

During the following seven years the disease spread inexorably throughout the country and in the autumn of 1915 R. W. Furze, the County Bee Inspector for

Devon, forecast that all the bees of the county would be dead by the spring. Brother Adam remembers local farmers and cottagers arriving at the abbey throughout the following summer with skeps full of dead and dying bees. This sorry course of events continued all summer.

From 1909, the Ministry of Agriculture had engaged a series of beekeepers and scientists to investigate this wholesale loss of bees which was beginning to affect the pollination of fruit crops as well as crippling commercial beekeepers. In the confusion and anxiety to solve the problem a variety of possibilities were named as culprit, among them the protozoan organism, *Nosema apis*. In addition to this many varied natural causes were blamed, poor weather, chemical sprays, poisonous plants and probably the most suspect, the movable-frame hive! This had been in use since the turn of the century and like all innovations was treated with mistrust.

It was not until A.H.E. Wood offered a grant of £500 per year for a period of five years, a sum matched by the Ministry of Agriculture, that Dr John Rennie in his detailed research discovered the tracheal mite, *Tarsonnemus woodi* to which the outbreak was ascribed. At this time the investigators had been unable to detect the presence of this organism in honeybees of either Europe or North America, nor indeed any closely allied hymenoptera, and so it was concluded that this was indeed the cause of the Isle of Wight disease. Brother Adam totally supported this view and has not changed his opinion over the years. He believes that the sudden appearance of the mite, now named *Acarapis Woodi* (Rennie) may perhaps be the result of a mutation from one of the many external mites found on honeybees the world over. This view has sparked off recurrent discussions with opposing beekeepers and scientists, and such exchanges are particularly pertinent today with the recent arrival of this mite in the United States of America.

The disease is still a problem in the British Isles, particularly in the damp salty Devon air which seems to well suit its requirements. The mature female acarine mite enters the first thoracic spiracle (breathing hole) of a young bee and then proceeds to lay eggs within the trachea (breathing tube). These develop into nymphs and after a series of moults mature into the adult form, feeding meanwhile on the blood of their host. The adult females may reappear externally on the bee and so pass from one honeybee to another spreading the disease. Fumigant acaricides are readily available for the control of this mite but Brother Adam never uses them as he does not wish to mask the susceptibility of certain lines, but would rather observe them so that he may breed a resistance to the infestation in his own strain.

During this period when many beekeepers lost all their stocks the abbey

THE BEEKEEPERS' GAZETTE

St. Mary's Abbey, Buckfast, Devon.

Our good friend, FATHER M. MASSÉ, who used to contribute frequently to our columns, has not continued that excellent practice since the great War called him to France, but we rejoice to know that he is well, and is now Superior of a French Monastery. and also that he has left a good substitute in FATHER B. ADAM, who writes as follows :—

DEAR SIR,—Many thanks for your kind offer to write about our queen-rearing business in your papers. I am sending you by registered post two blocks of our home apiaries. I am sorry not to be able to send you one of our out-apiaries Well, perhaps another time. All the bees were wiped out by I. O. W. in our district. Our bees are the only survivors of the disease During the last few seasons we sold a large number of nuclei and queens, but, owing to several reasons, we are unable to continue selling them, and we are now working a number of our stocks for honey production and the rest for rearing "the very best" queens. The past season turned out to be the most unfavourable for many years. But in spite of this, our best stocks have produced over 80 lbs. of heather honey. I think they would have yielded over 100 lbs. had I been able to supply them with combs instead of foundation. The honey flow was only of six days' duration, towards the end of August. I hope we may have once again a good season. FR. M. MASSÉ, who frequently contributed to your paper before the war, is at present Superior of one of our French Monasteries. During the Great War he was lecturing on beekeeping to the British troops in France. With all best wishes for the coming season. I am, yours, etc., B. ADAM.

The Abbey apiaries have earned a good reputation for their home-bred Italian queens. No "Goldens" are there ; they are considered "too soft" for the climate, not wintering well, nor do the Monks rely upon imported Italian queens, preferring to breed at home by minute selection and "by correct scientific principles." They do sometimes import queens, which are carefully tested in out-apiaries which are worked for honey production, and they claim that this method gives them "a unique selection," so that only the best are used to breed from.

We are pleased to present herewith a view of one of the home-apiaries, from which come the "Very Best" queens, advertised in another page.

Brother Adam's letter published in the *Beekeeper's Gazette*, March 1921 fared little better, as only 16 out of their original 45 colonies survived. These were all either of Italian or Carniolan origin mated at random with the local British Black drones. It is of interest to note that Brother Adam believes this was the time when the native bee, brown in colour but known as the British Black became extinct in its pure form. This theory was very much supported by W. Herrod-Hempsall who was Technical Advisor to the Ministry of Agriculture from 1917 to 1940. He, like Brother Adam, had worked with this 'British Black bee' in his early days but despite some thirty years of travelling every corner of the British Isles, lecturing and working with bees he could subsequently find no evidence of its existence. It is still mentioned enthusiastically in amateur circles today as being a thrifty vigorous species producing pure white cappings, but in fact it was very susceptible to brood diseases and acarine. It was also decidedly nervous, and few at the abbey in those early days escaped its sting. Indeed, in order to examine a colony, Adam would kneel carefully on the ground to one side of the hive and spread the skirts of his black habit around him like a tent on the grass, so that when he opened up the colony the tenacious defenders were not able to crawl up his legs and sting him.

The subsequent shortage of bees in the land, together with the realisation that the imported strains had shown definite resistance to acarine, led Brother Columban and Brother Adam to keep many European strains of *Apis mellifera* in their apiaries. It was decided by May 1916 to make up the severe losses by splitting the remaining 16 colonies and heading them with 30 Italian queens imported direct from that country. Despite the war this was done and fortune at last smiled on their endeavours. The resultant 45 colonies built up well and were able to take advantage of the excellent July weather and gathered a surplus of 5000lb (2,268kg) of honey. This was when the decision was made to increase the hives from 45 to 100 and forgo the crop of honey for the year so that by 1918 Buckfast was in an excellent position to commence the sale of Italian cross-queens and bees.

Brother Columban, although an excellent beekeeper, found the rigours of commercialism too great, but Adam took this in his stride and it was decided that in the following year he should take on full responsibility for the bees, Brother Columban concentrating on work in the kitchens. World War I had now come to an end and a battered Europe could now pause to lick its wounds. A generation of young men had been lost or torn in the fields of Flanders and it would take more than the passing of one Christmas to heal the scars. Honeybees were more easily replaced and 1919 dawned with the government, under the direction of Herrod-Hempsall, deciding upon a general restocking programme with Dutch bees throughout Britain. Thousands of packages of this brown 'Heath Bee', as it is commonly known, were sent to every corner of the land. It was a close relation of the original British Black bee and showed many of its characteristics, both good and bad, though not quite to the same degree.

Brother Adam therefore felt it was time to concentrate his efforts on honey production. The season was a very successful one showing a profit of some £300 with the sale of a number of nuclei and the chance development of an outstanding Italian X British Black queen. September saw a great shortage of sugar in Britain so that only a few of the colonies could be fed as required. In Adam's own words:

> "All the stocks were in good condition and when they were checked in October the weather was warm and sunny, truly a St. Luke's summer. Suddenly on the 21st of that month the temperature fell and by November the first snow lay on the ground. At the end of November the weather had become mild again and the bees were very active."

Adam therefore gambled and attempted to take advantage of this warm spell and completed the feeding, as sugar had now become more readily available. The very mild damp weather continued right through the spring and he remembers apple bursting into blossom as early as March. Sadly only three of the full-sized colonies which had been fed early in the year survived, the remainder suffering from severe dysentery which Adam felt was the result of the unavoidable late feeding. The nuclei which were given the more readily available bakers fondant sustained no losses.

Brother Adam however did not falter in the face of this early failure, and with continued support of the ever helpful Abbot Anscar was allowed to make good the losses. As we shall see he immediately set to work on the rebuilding and reorganisation of the stocks, hives, extraction plant, and apiaries in general.

For the Love of Bees

Chapter 4
A new Broom In The Bee Department

Each day Adam worked towards the final hurdle of his last profession when he would accept the rule of St Benedict. On that morning, before the morning Mass continued, he would read aloud his perpetual vows to the abbot and sign the parchment which lay on the altar. In those days the lay brothers did not have to complete the full ritual as did the choir monks who would lie prostrate before the altar, a black funeral pall covering them, a candle at their feet and another at their head while high above the abbey bell tolled their death to the world, though today no distinction is made between the ordained fathers and the brothers. Despite these rigid religious commitments Adam's zest for beekeeping remained steadfast. Then, as now, he felt that he had been chosen for the work and could best serve God and the community through his bees. His endeavours were to lead him along three distinct paths, the management of the bees and apiaries, the reorganisation and rebuilding of the extracting and bottling plant, and lastly the breeding of the honeybee for which he was to become famed.

This term 'breeding' is one Brother Adam has always reserved for the selection of queens from a large number of colonies and the subsequent production of their progeny under controlled mating conditions. This involves an actual genetic improvement of the stocks rather than simply raising new queens from a particular mother without regard to other factors.

Several writings and papers had been published since the advent of modern beekeeping methods but four or five outstanding contributors were to make a lasting impression on Adam. As early as 1898 Dr U. Kramer had set up an isolated station in Switzerland for the purpose of line breeding the black native Swiss bee. Brother Adam felt that success was limited because Dr Kramer neither tested the queens under normal conditions of honey production, nor had sufficient isolation for controlled mating. At that time only 1 mile (1.6km) radius was considered, quite erroneously, to be the maximum flying range for both queens and drones during mating.

Two beekeepers within the United Kingdom were also making noteworthy efforts in this field at the same time. Samuel Simmins, as previously mentioned, had achieved great success with his White Star queens, believed to be a cross of imported Carniolan-Cyprian stock, though his mating methods were somewhat haphazard. The other innovator was F. W. Sladen who was one of the first to apply the laws of heredity, as set out by the Augustinian monk Gregor Mendel in 1860, to the breeding of the honeybee. His findings concerning the 'British Golden Bee' were published in the *British Bee Journal* of 1912, the article being taken from a lecture delivered by him on the eve of his departure for Canada where he spent the last nine years of his life. Sladen had also found matings difficult to control but attempted to improve this, in later years, by the use of an island mating station at the eastern end of Lake Ontario. Alas his work was never completed owing to his untimely death in 1921.

The scientist who without doubt had the greatest influence on young Adam was Professor L. Armbruster whose theoretical approach to the breeding of the honeybee with regard to the laws of Mendel was set out in a paper entitled 'Bienenzucchtungskunde' ('Art of Bee Breeding') that Adam obtained in 1920. Armbruster was not a practical beekeeper but this never seemed to cause conflict with Adam's ideas, which has so often been the case. His erudite approach to life encompassed many fields, not least theology, as he was ordained a Catholic priest before he began his scientific studies. However his manner was full of humour and his appearance almost belied his priesthood as he rarely wore a dog collar and his mode of transport was a motorcycle. In 1933 he was forced into retirement from both his position as Director of the Bee Research Institute at Berlin-Dahlem and as editor of the *Archiv fur Bienenkunde*, by the Nazi regime with whom he openly disagreed. Hardship and poverty followed during the war years but on cessation of hostilities more articles on the breeding of the honeybee followed. These appeared at regular intervals in the *Archiv* until the time of his death in 1973.

Despite Adam's following of the professor's writings, it was not until 1950 that the two came face to face. They arranged to meet at Armbruster's home on the shores of Lake Constance which lay only 40 miles (64km) from Adam's birthplace near Biberach. Each was familiar with the other's work so the meeting was a great success and a strong friendship was formed. Armbruster was not only able to help Adam in his work in bee breeding, but by easing the way with the Italian authorities he was also instrumental in aiding the travels that Adam

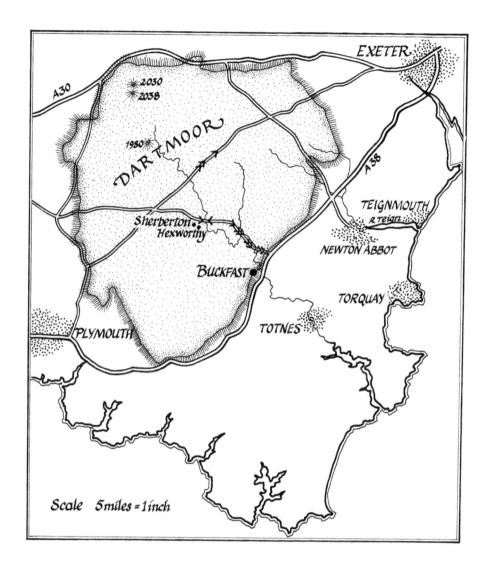

was later to undertake. Sadly Armbruster never visited the abbey at Buckfast. Arrangements had been made for him to return to England with Adam who was lecturing in Hanover in 1953, but ill-health forced the plan to be abandoned

Adam first attempted to control mating by keeping one type of drone in a particular apiary by providing each colony with a sister queen of identical origin. He felt that the continental method, whereby just a single drone-producing colony was kept in each apiary, was inadequate. Results proved his point, but the chance of mismatings remained and could only be eliminated by the use of an isolation apiary. He therefore decided to establish such a mating station on the same lines as the Swiss. The neighbouring area of high moorland, Dartmoor, seemed an obvious choice. Climatic conditions are harsh even in summer and in the winter for a period of four or five months the temperature rarely exceeds 50°F (10°C), combined with snow and heavy rainfall for much of the time. For example in early March of 1986 a record low of 26 degrees of frost was recorded.

This upland area consists of shallow peaty soil lying over granite outcrops that support few trees other than a small number of wind-torn, scraggy hawthorns. There are large tracts of wet spongy ground and it is these boggy areas that provide the source of such rivers as the Teign and the Dart. These flow rapidly from this highest point of the county which is about 1,200ft (365m) above sea level, to enter the sea at the centuries old ports of Teignmouth and Dartmouth. The waters of these moorland rivers, soft and brown from the peat through which they flow, are the home of trout and salmon and during periods of heavy rainfall are a most impressive sight when in spate - a white foam chuckling and tumbling over the polished granite boulders.

The flora of the high moors is fairly limited being in the main gorse (*Ulex europaeus*), the so-called Devon whortleberry (*Vaccinium myrtillus*) and the native heather or ling (*Calluna vulgaris*). There are a variety of bog plants and the ever increasing bracken but, from the beekeeper's point of view, the latter are without use. No wild colonies could survive unaided in these conditions, with scant supportive forage and the few twisted hawthorns that exist, bent and stunted in the south westerly winds, could not give any warm dry hollow shelter for a nest. After studying local maps Adam favoured a particularly desolate area that lay between Dartmeet and the road westwards to Two Bridges, so he set out in the pony and trap to investigate.

His searching brought him directly to a place called Sherberton which was to prove ideal in that it was both isolated and yet afforded a little shelter, but at the same time was not too far from the abbey. The farm was part of the extensive estates belonging to the Duchy of Cornwall. The tenant was Mr Frank Coker who had spent many months in hospital in Kingsbridge recovering from wounds received during World War I and whilst there had gained solace from the prior of Wood Barton, a local monastery of the Cistercian Order. Brother Adam was therefore made most welcome by the Cokers, a friendship which lasts to this day, and in 1925 the Sherberton mating apiary was established. At first, stands for the hives were positioned along the lower wall extending into the far end of the wood, but in later years as the trees became taller the higher ground was cleared and utilised as we see it today.

Co-operation was also sought from the members of the Devon Beekeepers' Association who agreed not to take bees to the heather at Brimpts Farm as they had done previously which was within the five-mile radius of the isolation area. Sherberton mating station was thus ready to be the base from which the bee breeding programme for the next fifty years would be executed, so a watchful eye for other hives in the vicinity would be always prudent.

Then, as now, two wooden footbridges crossed the fast-flowing moorland streams of the Swincombe river that separated the road from the apiary itself. In the spring a mass of bluebells and daffodils nod amongst the hives that are dotted about between the outcrops of granite - an idyllic scene, but even here disaster can strike. In 1932 Brother Adam with the aid of Father Benedict had transported two hundred nuclei to the mating station. Having started very early in the morning, they decided to have a cup of tea before unloading the van. They sat on the steps of the bee house enjoying their 'morning cuppa' in the sunshine when they suddenly became aware of a wisp of smoke drifting up from the van which stood some 200yd (180m) away on the flat ground next to the road. Cassocks flying they sped across the narrow planks that spanned the river. By the time they reached the van the flames had already engulfed the interior; the wood and wax of the combs and nucleus boxes were all blazing hotly. All they could do was stand and watch from a safe distance for fear of an explosion and in ten minutes it was all over. The blackened shell of the van was all that remained of the funeral pyre. A sorry sight indeed and a year's work lost.

At the same time as these developments were taking place Adam was also anxious to standardise all equipment for ease of working. In 1920 he had been one of the first to introduce to England the North American idea of wooden crown boards in place of the cloths and quilts in common use at that time. Most of the hives were Burgess Perfection but floors and crownboards were often made from makeshift timber or old packing cases as supplies of wood were very short so soon after the end of the war. Roofs too were fashioned in the same way and covered with a single sheet of pluvex roofing-felt with newspaper sandwiched between the crown board and roof to aid insulation and prevent heat loss. At times Adam feared that his plans were never to be fulfilled but providence always seemed to take a hand and the required materials were obtained from one source or another. Even the nails he used were ones that had been removed from the boxes in which groceries were delivered.

Adam felt very much that the ten British Standard frames in the brood box of the Perfection hive were inadequate for the' prolific Ligurian queens he had imported direct from the famous Penna Apiaries of Bologna. In 1920, therefore, he first tried running a colony on a double brood box. Throughout the season this stock seemed in advance of the others, filling 6 honey supers and finishing with a surplus of 1.5cwt (76kg)-40lb (18kg) greater than any other colony. This was his loadstar that would eventually lead him to the Dadant hive. Most progressive beekeepers at this time favoured the 10-framed Langstroth hive which gave a brood area of 1,371sq in (8, 845cm2), which Adam felt was still too small as compared with the 2, 126sq in (13,716cm2) of a double British Standard brood box. His reservations on using the double box stemmed from the fact that the space between the boxes presented a barrier to a laying queen and therefore tended to restrict the brood area artificially. Also the extra time taken in working two brood boxes had to be considered in a commercial situation.

In 1923 an article in the American journal *Gleanings* caught his eye and he decided to import the first six modified Dadant hives to be used in Britain. These were sent over in the 'flat' and, when assembled, produced a square brood box of just under 20 X 20 X 12in (50 X 50 X 30cm) that gave a brood area of 2,050 sq in (13,225cm2) over the 12 frames.

These simple hives were not identical to those used in the States but had some modifications which are still incorporated today. The sturdy boxes are rebated in order to hold them together more firmly and they have a bottom bee space which is the more common practice in Britain. The bottom boards extend 1 inch (2.5cm) at the front and incorporate a slope to prevent rain collecting and to facilitate removal of debris by the bees. All the frames are of wide top bar design which reduces the building of brace comb and propolis, and the spacing of these was effected by the use of hobnails which were, at that time, readily available from Messrs Burgess in Exeter. Brother Adam was so pleased with this system of spacing that although such nails are no longer available he arranged, in 1985, for identical plastic studs to be fabricated at the factory of his long-time friend Heff Zimmer of Alsace.

The first 'out apiary' had been established at Staverton Bridge Farm in 1920 and four years later the number of such sites had risen to 3, each containing about 40 colonies. It was decided that year to transfer half the colonies in each apiary into the new Modified Dadant hive. That year proved a poor one, all the colonies having little surplus honey, and the start of the following year, 1925, seemed no better, Suddenly in June the weather changed and continuous sunshine at last arrived. These simple solid hives proved their worth with a surplus of3cwt (152kg) of honey from the best Dadant hive as compared with just under 2cwt (102kg) from the best British Standard. Adam had feared that the large brood boxes would prove unsuitable for the heather crop as most local beekeepers predicted that the honey would be stored in the brood box rather than the supers. He was delighted to find that this was not the case, an average of 100lb (45kg) per colony being extracted.

It was therefore decided to complete the changeover to the new hives and gradually the double-walled hives were phased out, the lines of inner boxes no longer being a feature of the moorland scene. The cost of the new hives was covered by the sale of the remaining WBC and Perfection hives together with their stocks, the work being finally completed in 1930.

It was at about this time that the abbey wanted to extend the small cemetery and it was decided that the adjacent home apiary should be moved to give room for the necessary expansion. The present site was chosen; it lies adjacent to the River Dart at a point where the weir spans the river, taking the water to feed the leat which ran directly behind the abbey itself and thence to the woollen mills situated behind the workshops, The waters in those days were extremely pure and well stocked with fish. It was a common sight to see salmon-trout lying on the banks with one clean bite removed from their backs where the otters, now rarely seen in Devon, had been successful in their ravages of the previous night. One August when the salmon were travelling up river to spawn and the weather had been exceptionally hot and dry so that there was insufficient water over the weir to allow their passage upstream, Adam clearly remembers counting 73 fish within 1/4 mile (.4km) stretch of the river.

Over the winter of 1929-30 the chosen area was turfed and laid out with flower-beds and the queen rearing house moved to its new position. Adam designed and then built four large bee huts measuring 8 X 11 ft (2.4 x 3.3m) which were then erected at each of the out apiaries and one at the entrance to the home apiary. These were constructed in wood in nine sections so that they could be assembled and bolted together on site making it possible, if necessary, for them to be moved at a later date. These same huts are still in use today and still in excellent condition.

It was quite by chance that Mr Mavie, a beekeeper from Winchester in the south of England. decided at this time to visit Buckfast with his wife, He had been medically advised to take up an outdoor job following a severe illness and had chosen beekeeping. Naturally enough Brother Adam was the obvious source from which to glean some knowledge of the commercial aspects of the craft. A friendship soon developed as both parties were interested in breeding. Daffodils were the love of John Mavie and from a few special varieties such as 'White Nile' which were a gift, and one or two more that he purchased, Adam was able to produce his own hybrid seedlings. Huge white blooms with pink trumpets, and brilliant orange and yellow narcissi, a legacy of those early efforts, still grace the home apiary and the Sherberton mating station every spring.

Adam also discussed the planting of the flower beds in the new home apiary and expressed an interest in tuberous rooted begonias. No sooner said than done; Mavie obtained 1,000 tubers of a single variety direct from Paris and presented them to the abbey. For two years Adam grew them with pride but in the autumn of 1932 the waxy blooms were so magnificent that he delayed lifting them for the winter period for just a week or so. Clearly Adam recalls the series of events that followed. 'It was the 22nd October 1932 and the moon was huge, quite full, and we suffered the severest frost of the winter which can happen once the 20th of the month is passed. All the tubers, every one, were lost.' Mavie replaced the tubers but in 1941 Adam decided to purchase seeds from Blackmore & Langdon in Somerset and raise his own. He selected the best dozen from the 2,500 plants he raised and then multiplied these by propagating cuttings. The result was quite breathtaking and once again shows his flair for breeding and selection.

Over the years little has changed in the abbey apiaries. Then, as now, to prevent drifting, the hives were placed in groups of four, each of the entrances facing a different direction and the hive stands arranged so that the brood chambers were always 2ft (.6km) off the ground for ease of working. Modern methods of agriculture have meant a substantial loss of bee forage. For example the system of monoculture where large areas are laid down to one crop, usually corn, and the increased heavy application of nitrogen to improve grass yields has resulted in the reduction of wild white clover in permanent pasture. Similarly the destruction of hedgerows, whilst those remaining are cut with flail mowers, has meant the removal of much wild flower particularly blackthorn, hawthorn, sallow and blackberry. This in turn has reduced the number of colonies that can be supported in a given area. Whereas at times up to 100 stocks could be found at one of the abbey out apiaries in the 1930s this had dropped to 40 after World War II and by 1970 was reduced still further, standing at about 20 today in most apiaries.

This large increase in the number of colonies meant that Adam also had to find a more efficient way of feeding the bees. Before 1917 soft candy made from honey was used for feeding, in fact Brother Columban was regarded as an expert on the subject (see also page 88). Not only did his recipe for this appear in the *British Bee Journal* of September 1905, but reports of his judgement and helpful criticism of other beekeepers' attempts, together with recipes for honey cakes and other confectionery items. followed in later issues. After 1917 Adam began using sugar syrup which he fed to the bees from 28lb (12.6kg) tins inverted over the hive. These proved somewhat unstable and if there was a sudden rise in temperature following an early morning chill the vacuum would be lost and the syrup would leak.

He persisted with this method until 1932 when a stormy autumn night wreaked havoc among the colonies. The sight of scattered lifts and syrup sodden bees prompted Adam to design and make a tray feeder which was to be patented in his name and is still in use today. It was made of 7/8in (22mm)

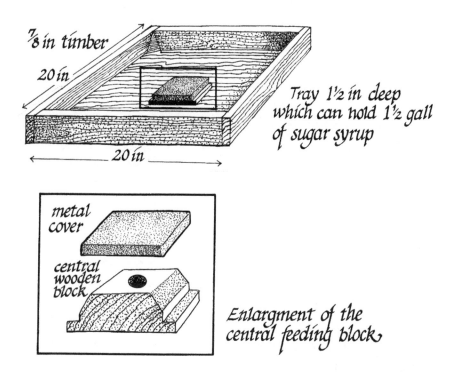

Tray 1½ in deep which can hold 1½ gall of sugar syrup

Enlargment of the central feeding block

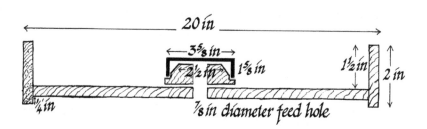

timber, reinforced at the corners for extra strength. The whole was completely waterproofed by immersing it totally in hot paraffin wax. The central feed block was fitted with a tin cover that allowed the bees to entirely clean up the 1.5gal (6.8 litres) of syrup while both the crown board and roof fitted over it exactly and so prevented any danger of robbing.

Before 1932 the syrup was mixed in a copper boiler and feeding had to be carried out at night so as not to excite the bees. All this necessitated a great deal of work and was a most irksome task. That year Adam designed and built a glazed, tiled, rectangular mixing tank that would hold 1.5 tons (tonnes) of sugar. It was possible to mix this sugar with cold water quite satisfactorily using a 16in (40cm) wide stainless steel paddle. The process now took only about fifteen minutes and although the finished syrup still appeared a little cloudy no problems occurred as long as the sugar was not allowed to settle. The syrup was then pumped directly into cradled tanks in the van waiting outside and feeding could then be carried out at any time without fear of robbing which is always a threat.

In 1921 when a surplus of approximately 9 tons(tonnes) of clover honey was obtained from 160 colonies, all the apparatus for extracting honey was situated on the first floor of the present building. It was therefore necessary to carry every full super, each weighing 20-30lbs (9-13kg), up to the top of the narrow winding staircase. The extraction was carried out with a small hand extractor which had been purchased a couple of years earlier, the old single two-frame one being quite inadequate. The process was still painfully slow and the work of extraction continued late into November despite Adam working well into the night.

Initially the honey was stored in glass accumulator jars but this was found to be unsatisfactory as the honey granulated and sometimes the glass cracked and creating a problematical mass of honey and broken glass. Subsequently homemade tanks lined with tin were tried. The tin was of poor quality due to the postwar shortage of metal and these too sometimes split. It was therefore evident that drastic alterations would have to be made to the extraction and storage plant and so wheels were put in motion to make the essential changes.

Later in 1930 A.W.Gale of Marlborough in Wiltshire, a longstanding personal friend who was one of the largest producers of honey in Britain at that time, loaned Adam a newly acquired bottling machine. This proved most satisfactory and was subsequently purchased at a cost of £40. This same machine is still in use today though for economic reasons plastic containers are used now instead of the waxed cardboard pots for which it was originally designed.

The extraction of the late heather honey, which was taken from the high

A new Broom In The Bee Department

An advertisement for Gale's Honey

areas of Dartmoor not far from Buckfast, was an important source of revenue for the abbey and was to present even more of a problem. This honey from the true heather, the ling heath *Callulla vulgaris*, exhibits strange thixotropic qualities similar to non-drip paint. This property which is peculiar to heather honey and manuka honey from New Zealand, is ascribed to the content of certain proteins within the honey which do not allow it to flow sufficiently to be extracted in conventional centrifugal extractors without prior agitation. Alternatively the honey may be pressed from the comb itself, and a small Steele & Brodie hand press had been used for this until 1925 when the screw finally gave out. This had only been able to handle four super combs cut from the frames at each pressing and the work was painfully slow.

A wine press was now brought into use which gave a pressure of some 5-6 tons (tonnes), but this also proved inadequate for the job. In November 1925, therefore, an old wooden cider press made for Whiteways in Somerset was installed. There was already frost on the ground and the low temperature meant the honey was so thick that it would not pass through the press but oozed out of the sides. Brother Adam recalls the horrified expressions on the faces of the Benedictine sisters from Chudleigh who had broken their journey at Buckfast during their move to nearby Syon Abbey at South Brent. Their visit to the honey department coincided with the sticky mess spreading out over the floor and they left rapidly muttering graciously 'It looks so dirty but we know it isn't!'

Originally six men were needed to work the press but when once it was converted to electricity Adam could complete the work on his own if need be. Herrod-Hempsall in his two epic volumes on beekeeping describes it as 'the best and most powerful press it has been our pleasure to see' and goes on to elaborate on its workings. It is sufficient here to say that the combs, having been cut from the frames, were wrapped in cheesecloth and rested on top of 20 iron bars that formed a grid across 4 steel joists. The wooden pressing board was swung into position and a series of gear wheels gave a range of 4 speeds to assist reaching a maximum pressure of some 8 tons(tonnes). The body of the press consisted of 3ft (1m) thick concrete in order to withstand the immense pressure and the whole was finished in spotless white enamelled bricks. A tank that held 5cwt (254kg) of honey was incorporated into the press to allow for the temporary storage of the extracted crop.

The apparatus however remained temperamental and inefficient, and by weighing the resultant rendered wax from the pressings Adam estimated that some 20 per cent of the honey was being lost. Finally in 1927 Adam allowed his attention to wander whilst operating the machine and the press itself cracked.

Immediately he formulated the basic plans for an hydraulic press along the lines of the old cider press, but which would give a pressure of up to 100 tons (tonnes). He then approached a young draughtsman on the staff of Willcocks & Son Foundry in Buckfastleigh who were already engaged in making a cider press for Whiteways Cider Company. Within six months the plans had been drawn up and a prototype completed. There were one or two teething problems but these were soon rectified. Firstly the iron counterweights had to be replaced with lead ones as the mechanism lacked weight; then a heavy-gauge gauze had to be used between the cloths that enveloped the stack of ten super combs and the pressing grid, otherwise the cloths split immediately pressure was applied. Even following these modifications the cheesecloth that was used before 1940 would only last a couple of pressings. Today nylon cloths, as used in the china clay industry, last almost indefinitely.

Brother Adam estimates, from experiments he has made comparing the weight of the old pressed comb against the total weight of the rendered wax, the dross and the wires, that the maximum pressure of 2cwt per sq in (31kg/cm^2), together with the steam-heating of the components, extracts 98 per cent of the honey and that 2 tons(tonnes) of heather honey can be extracted in one day. A stack of 10 super combs is soon reduced to a wafer of wax barely 1/2in (12mm) thick. This press is still in service and completes a hard week's work every September, having been trouble free for the last quarter of a century.

Gradually the equipment had taken on a modern shape and Adam could turn his attention to the building itself. He himself made 11 storage tanks, completely lined with tin and capable of holding a total of 27.5 tons (tonnes) of honey. Each has its own pipe work to warm the stored honey connected directly to a boiler downstairs by 1in (2.5cm) piping. Rows of varnished red deal boxes line the walls each holding 20lb (9kg) of jarred honey ready for sale. All this was fashioned by Brother Adam himself from rough sawn timber, sheet tin and lengths of copper pipe. He would toil late into the night long after his normal day's work had finished and would often be retiring as the choir monks rose to say the morning office, only to rise again at 5am. One only has to step into the honey house today to wonder at the carpentry and metal-work completed by one man. Even more remarkable is the fact that the only change he would make after all these years would be to use stainless steel instead of the sheet tin then available. The arrangements thought out and planned so many years ago are still quite suitable today.

The work took its toll however and in January 1932 Adam fell ill and suffered his first breakdown. This, together with the news that his father had died the previous year, made him decide to return home to Germany for three months. But he felt compelled to return to his duties with the bees in the spring, despite

A. W. Gale's generous offer of supervising the work on them in his absence. He was to return home again at the beginning of 1939 as his mother was seriously ill. This was the first occasion that Adam remembered seeing his cousin Maria, a little girl of nine and a favorite of his mother. Adam found the situation in Germany at that time very disturbing as Nazi indoctrination was everywhere and was already a part of every school curriculum. He was also concerned for his mother's safety as her reluctance to hang the ubiquitous red and black banner from her balcony had met with strong disapproval. His fears that war was imminent were confirmed later that year when Hitler's armies marched into Poland.

That very winter of 1939 Adam was again forced to his bed and remained there from Christmas until Easter. The doctor diagnosed a "heart disorder caused by overwork and said that he would never work again. Adam endeavoured to survey the rebuilding programme for half an hour each day as the plans were entirely his own and he wished to see they were being followed exactly. A new outer staircase had been erected in the extracting area and in 1940 the mosaic tiled floor was laid. The work was finally complete and Adam could be well satisfied.

Chapter 5
Planning Ahead For The Perfect Bee

The period of Brother Adam's convalescence dragged on and, hollow cheeked and thin, he had lost all zest for life. In November 1940 it was decided that he should take up the invitation of his friends Mr and Mrs Mavie and spend some time with them at their new home in Little Strickland, Westmorland. They had decided to leave Hampshire at the start of the war and Mr Mavie now ran some two hundred colonies on the moors of the border counties in the north of England

Brother Adam took his books with him and in the evenings studied in front of the fire. He read extensively on all aspects of beekeeping in journals and publications from both home and abroad. He contemplated the works of D.A. Jones and Frank Benton who had endeavoured to find a superior race of honeybee by travelling extensively in Europe in 1880 and 1882. He also examined the work of Dr Goetze of Germany who had listed the different characteristics of races of honeybees, but based on hearsay and the behaviour patterns of imported specimens, and not on bees studied in their natural environment.

Adam pored over the papers of Professor Armbruster and saw the exciting possibilities of breeding a quieter, more industrious and productive honeybee from pure stocks of different races. Mavie was full of enthusiasm for this idea and felt that Adam should himself travel to obtain both first-hand experience and samples of these various races. He was convinced that such work would be accepted world wide and that Adam must make plans for an expedition without delay. Adam himself doubted the possibility of attempting such work. There were a number of problems. War raged in Europe at that time and Adam had no way of knowing how such a venture would be received by the abbot and his colleagues at Buckfast. However the seeds had been sown and these thoughts and ideas would not be dispelled for the rest of his life.

He already had an immense knowledge of the different races of bees and his wealth of experience as a beekeeper was recognised in England. As early as 1929 he had been invited to lecture at the first Beekeepers' National Congress which was held at Seale Hayne Agricultural College, Newton Abbot, towards the end of that year. The subject was 'Out Apiaries and their Management' and in his lecture he stressed the necessity for annual re-queening and the merits of the leather-coloured Italian bee. It was arranged that the delegates should visit the abbey apiaries the following day. Glowing reports appeared in the September edition of the *British Bee Journal* and the article describing Adam as having an unostentatious manner went on: 'Like the bees he never appears to sleep in the summer, with apiary work, invention and experimentation he is one of nature's silent workers and the most competent one in Great Britain.' Ten years later he was invited to serve on the Ministry of Agriculture advisory committee on apiculture. He attended quarterly meetings at Rothamsted which inevitably brought him into contact with many of the leading beekeepers throughout Europe.

From Westmorland, Adam returned to the abbey where the community was playing its part in the wartime effort of increasing food production, which included honey. But at the same time there were many 'prejudiced' opinions being voiced against minority groups and Buckfast was, on occasions, such a target. Wild stories again filled the air as they had in World War I and Adam himself was accused of arranging his hives on the moor in such a pattern so as to point out the direction of Plymouth to the attacking Luftwaffe!

The Home Guard under the direction of Major Pearce vigilantly checked travellers journeying across the moor by road, whilst a separate group, the Moorland Patrol, surveyed the remote windswept uplands on horseback. It so happened one September morning that Adam and several of his brethren were transporting bees back from the heather on the west side of the moor to an apiary near Buckfast when they were stopped and questioned by a Home Guard patrol. Unfortunately three of the monks had failed to carry their identity cards and were immediately arrested and confined to a room in the nearby inn at Postbridge. The police headquarters at HM Prison Dartmoor, Princetown, were informed of the action later in the day and an officer was sent to investigate. It was not until late that evening that the whole unnecessary matter was sorted out.

After the war, in 1947, because of the poor state of his mother's health, Adam decided to return to Germany again. Eight years had passed since he had last seen his home and in that time much had changed. Three years earlier in 1944 both his brothers had died, the younger one Friedrich tragically

(above) 1906: the ruins of the medieval abbey were discovered in the vegetable garden and it was decided to rebuild on the existing foundations, incorporating the Abbot's Tower" (below) the Abbey Church, 1930, viewed from the home apiary.

(above) The roof tops of Biberach, Brother Adam's home town in Southern Germany;
(below) Adam (front row, second from the right) with the other new arrivals in 1910 was to serve as one of 24 pupils in the alumnate.

Adam managed to keep his three rabbits in the greenhouse quite successfully and after twelve months they numbered more than a dozen.

(above) 1912 several of the novices, Adam included, would work long hours butting and dressing the blocks of stone; (below) Brother Columban at work in the apiary beside the canal in 1905, when most of the huge double-.walled hives were of French origin and of all shapes and sizes.

1914: Brother Columban takes a swarm.

(above) Holme Moor, 1920; the lines of makeshift hives, used until 1930, were a familiar sight on Dartmoor in August when the bees were taken to the heather; (below) 1925: the first year that the lorry belonging to the Co-operative Society Ltd, Buckfastleigh, was used for transportation of the bees

(above) 1923 saw a good crop of honey judging by the numbers of supers on the hives and the delighted faces of the beekeepers; (below) September 1949: the first of many visit to Buckfast by Mr. W. Herod-Hempsall.

Prof L. Armbruster was without doubt the scientist who had the greatest influence on young Adam with regard to the breeding of the honeybee.

(above) the honey cartons exquisitely designed in pastel shades by Brother Gabriel and used form 1926 until 1972; (below) the hand-operated heather press, installed in October 1926, was adapted from an old cider press and later converted to power.

A portrait of Adam in his thirties (1933).

(above) Egypt 1962: The clay pipe hives are just piled together, sometimes in their hundreds, merely sheltered from the direct sun at midday by a layer of clay or a mat of rushes; (below) a battery of hornet traps sited beside a modern apiary in an attempt to reduce the numbers of the marauding attackers.

(above) Vld Dermatoupolis accompanied Brother Adam in 1981 on his memorable trip to Athos.

(left) Tanzania 1987: the log hives, some five feet in length, are suspended high up in the trees.

Brother Adam and the author together with Mr Liana Hassan, director of the beekeeping unit of the Serengeti Wildlife Institute, Tanzania.

The famous mating station in Sherberton, Dartmoor, which has been the centre of all the breeding work since it was established in 1925.

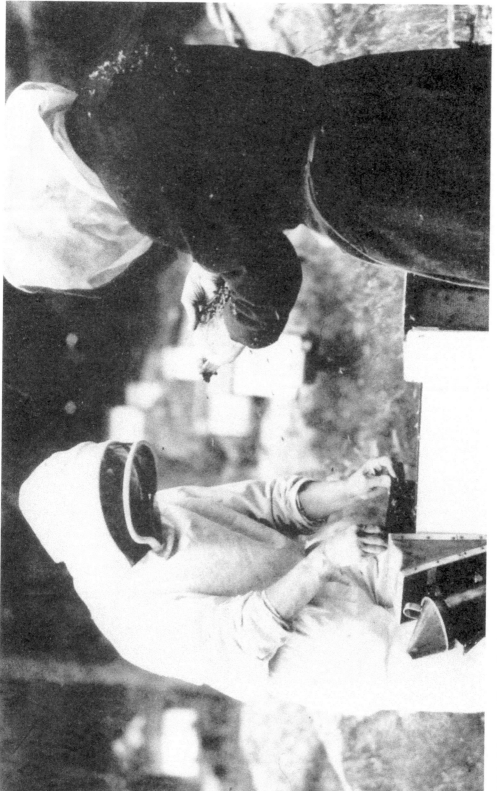

Brother Adam and the author hard at work in the preparation of the nucleus hives prior to the distribution of the queen cells.

Adam in later years.

killed in an Allied air raid. Württemberg was still under French occupation and Adam had to arrange for a special pass and the necessary food coupons, which he did without too much difficulty. The condition of Frau Kehrle was very grave and Adam decided he must prolong his stay. This necessitated an extension of his pass, which meant travelling to Tubingen to obtain it. There was no public transport at the time and the only mode of travel was on the lorry that made the weekly deliveries of wood. The vehicle groaned in the early morning blackness as it drew to a halt at the prearranged meeting point. The cab was already full to bursting with other would-be travellers and there was nothing for it but for Adam to perch on top of the load. Alas, after a long cold uncomfortable journey, the officials at Tubingen were unable to help.

Adam was not to be deterred by this setback so from there he journeyed by rail to Friedrichshafen, which lay in ruins after repeated attacks by the Allied forces. Then after a roundabout route and many hours of waiting for trains which never seemed to arrive he found himself in Baden-Baden. Here he could obtain the extension pass but even then it took another three days to complete the paperwork during which time he was offered the hospitality of a nearby convent. This episode shows clearly his determination in attaining a goal and his casual attitude to travel under extreme difficulties, both qualities essential for the work ahead.

Adam returned home to his mother who was overjoyed as she had been convinced that he had been forced to return to England. She seemed to recover a little in the weeks that followed so he eventually returned to Buckfast. Sadly she died some ten day's after his departure and his cousin Maria wrote and told him of the sad news. From then on Maria became a regular correspondent and a warm friendship followed that is still valued by both of them today. She is a religious, well-read and hospitable soul who enjoys life to the full even lending a hand with a pitchfork on the adjoining family farm. Her own interest in bees grew with her friendship with her cousin and she still maintains eight stocks of Buckfast bees at her home in Mittel Biberach. Her convivial personality makes her an excellent companion and on many occasions she has generously put her home at the disposal of Brother Adam and his friends on their visits to Germany.

Mr. Mavie had not forgotten the idea of investigating the different races of bees and now, in 1948, twelve months after the death of Adam's mother, and with some degree of normality returning to the countries bordering the Mediterranean, he wrote to Abbot Bruno Fehrenbacher. Lengthy discussions between the elders of the abbey followed as at that time the community was not so able to mix with the general populace as it is now. Some felt it was not the role of a monk to be singled out from his brethren, whilst others felt that the improvement in stocks and subsequent honey revenues would not be commensurate with the expense incurred. Yet the work was important, and a favourable response was eventually conveyed to Adam giving him the confidence to begin planning his journeys.

He had started writing a book entitled *Bee-keeping at Buckfast Abbey* some years earlier in response to a request from a London publisher. Everyone was anxious for the volume to be completed but Adam felt that the writing could wait and nothing should delay the expedition. He later attended the International Congress in Amsterdam in 1949 where he met others who were interested in bee breeding. Lasting friendships ensued from this gathering and several of the acquaintances were instrumental in providing bases for Adam during his journeys. The date was set; he was to commence his travels in the spring of 1950.

The Ministry of Agriculture was notified of his intentions and they gave him their full support. They recommended that a new car would be essential for such a demanding journey which was planned to take approximately six months. At that time only doctors and midwives were eligible for new vehicles owing to a shortage in the postwar years. It was also agreed that Brother Adam would be able to issue his own health certificates for the importation of bees. Later special arrangements were made with the Customs and Excise at Heathrow Airport, London, so that any consignments of bees would be sent on to Buckfast without delay. On their arrival at the abbey Brother Pascal introduced the queens to the waiting nuclei and the accompanying workers were despatched to Rothamsted for analysis to eliminate the possibility of disease being introduced to this country from far-off lands.

Financial co-operation had also to be obtained from the Bank of England as at that time a limit of £80 sterling was all that one was permitted to take out of the country which was of course totally insufficient. The Bee Department of Buckfast Abbey financed the whole operation at a cost of £400, a figure that by today's inflated standards seems remarkably little.

The first journey began modestly on 20 March 1950 with Adam setting out quite alone in his Austin A40. The car was filled with veil, smoker, smoker fuel and the numerous boxes that in due course would be needed for the samples he was to collect for the Bee Department of Rothamsted Experimental Station at Harpenden as well as his own cages for his collection of sample queens.

It is beyond the scope of this book to detail the complete itinerary or the findings of such a mission. Brother Adam has himself published a full account entitled In *Search of the Best Strains of Bees*. Even thirty years ago he describes "the many strains he encountered as a mishmash of American-bred Italian queens crossed with local drones so that each native bee was hard to find. How much more difficult this task would be today. In the time that has elapsed transport and communications have reached all corners of Europe and only a few pockets of isolated pure strains are to be found anywhere in this region. Coupled with the necessarily strict regulations on the importation of bees due to the advent of such disease problems as varroasis this important collection, evaluation and subsequent breeding and crossbreeding of different strains of bees could no longer be carried through in the same way.

Having crossed the English Channel from Newhaven Brother Adam travelled south from Dieppe to the Mediterranean coast of France where he tells us the rosemary and white clover were in full bloom despite it being the last week of March. Taking advantage of the milder climate, he spent the first few weeks investigating the 'native vile tempered bee of France'. In this windy region of the Corbieres and the neighbouring Spanish border country he found some of the best examples of this particular bee.

In April he travelled to Switzerland where he was anxious to visit the Liebefeld Institute of Berne which was without doubt the leading centre of beekeeping research in Europe at that time. Professor Morgenthaler was the Director, another scientist who also had an impact on Adam's thinking during his formative years. He specialised in bee diseases, particularly acarine, an interest shared by Brother Adam, as we have already seen in his quest to overcome the effects of the Isle of Wight disease. Prior to his death in 1973, the same year as Professor Armbruster, he had become the first secretary and later the first president of the International Bee Congress, Apimondia.

Unfortunately Professor Morgenthaler was absent on this occasion but Dr Anna Maurizio, whom Adam had met in Amsterdam the previous year, was able to introduce him to both her own work on pollen analysis and the extensive efforts that the department was making into the attempted eradication of acarine disease in Switzerland. The work in which Adam was particularly interested was that of Herr Fyg who was studying the anatomy and physiology and allied pathology of queen honeybees, as his own practical experience in this field had left many unanswered questions. This first visit to Switzerland was a short one but Adam was to return three times in all that year.

He had arranged to visit the beekeepers of Carinthia, north-western Yugoslavia, but en route into Austria he passed by both his home town of Biberach and also Lindau on the shore of Lake Constance which happened to be the home of Professor Armbruster. The opportunity was not to be missed and having spent Easter with his cousin Maria, Brother Adam was at last able to meet the great man. He had followed the work of Armbruster with great zeal and their common aim was to breed a bee that would produce maximum returns with a minimum of labour. The articles on bee genetics published in *Archiv für Bienenkunde* had been the inspiration that had set Adam on the road to his own particular goal. The meeting was successful and was to be the first of many. In fact on the return journey Armbruster, acting as guide, accompanied Adam on his exploration of the Algau, the area surrounding Lindau.

It was well into April before he reached Carinthia. It had been quite a hazardous journey as wintery conditions still prevailed as he crossed the Voralberg Pass from south Germany into Austria. At one point the car had come to a slippery silent halt. Fortunately a party of skiers based on the other side of the mountain had chosen these slopes for their sport and had observed Adam's plight. Two of the men volunteered to shovel away the snow and they were then able to push the car out of the snowdrift and back on course.

This corner where Austria met north-west Yugoslavia was one of the main areas of distribution of the renowned grey Carnica bee, famed for its extreme gentleness. This bee has always been known as the Carniolan in England as the first importations of this race came from the area of Carniola. Snow-clad mountains all the year round provided natural barriers which had created totally isolated pockets that encouraged pure matings and natural selection. In this region therefore there was a wealth of pure strains each differing slightly from those in the neighbouring valleys and which required considerable investigation. Adam was therefore fortunate in receiving the hospitality of the local parish priest whilst he completed this work. He felt that these bees, as also the original ones that Brother Columban had imported direct from the famous apiaries of Michael Ambrozic of Moistrana in Upper Carniola, were far less inclined to swarm than those produced by the continental beekeepers of today.

The days were now longer and a little warmer and as Adam retraced his steps through Austria, south Germany and Switzerland he was able to study the Central European brown bee and the related alpine varieties including the jet black Nigra of the Swiss Alps. The return journey was made all the more worthwhile as Professor Morgenthaler and two of his colleagues from the breeding department of the Berne Institute organised and accompanied him on his journey through Switzerland. They concentrated on the German-speaking districts of the country which also gave Adam a chance to study the heavily timbered bee houses of the area which are often finely carved with elaborate themes. Besides being a brilliant biologist in the field of bee diseases Morgenthaler realised the importance of the practical application of his work. He insisted his students spent a period of time with a commercial beekeeper before they began work in the laboratory, an attitude highly praised by Brother Adam.

At each stage of the journey, honeybee samples were prepared for the Rothamsted Experimental Bee Research Unit under the direction of Dr Colin Butler whom Adam had first met in 1939 when Dr Butler was appointed head of the Entomology and Bee Research team. At that time Adam agreed to aid their experimental programme firstly by supplying breeding stock to improve their strain of bee and secondly by agreeing to send them the 200 or so discarded old queens that had headed the honey production colonies at Buckfast prior to the annual requeening. Over the years more than 1,500 live queens must have been supplied gratis to Rothamsted for experimental purposes. Dr Butler was hoping to undertake a series of biometric measurements relating to the varying races of the honeybee. The bees were killed in boiling water and then carefully labelled and stored in the bottles of alcohol that Adam had brought with him. Some of these results were published by Elizabeth Carlisle in 1955 but this work was never completed in Britain as the ministry team had immersed itself in the well documented research of queen pheromones. The morphometric samples were not wasted however as Dr F. Ruttner of Oberusel heard of this work and approached Brother Adam at the International Bee Congress in Madrid in 1961 as to the possibility of using a portion of the sample material. Dr Butler agreed and Ruttner's initial data supported Adam's theory of the origins and distribution of the races of *Apis mellifera* in Europe and their glacial-barrier isolation during the Ice Age. It was not until the seventies that the remaining samples held at Rothamsted were finally relinquished. In Dr Ruttner's own words:

> "Brother Adam's precious collection, correctly preserved and labelled, furnished the basis of the morphometric data bank of the Institute of Apicultural Research Oberusel, University of Frankfurt, which comprises of more than 1,300 honeybee samples that are no longer available in consequence of later hybridization (e.g. bees of Israel and Turkey). The final results of the analyses carried out with this large collection is a book entitled 'Biogeography and Taxonomy of Honeybees' which is to be published by the end of 1987."

Adam's own work, on his journey, of obtaining breeding material was often more difficult as beekeepers are usually loath to part with good queens whatever the incentive may be. However with his usual quiet manner and dogged determination he successfully collected breeding material and despatched it with due haste to England. The work for the present came to a halt as the long days of the English summer and the golden harvest at Buckfast called him back to Devon. There was much to do. The way ahead was quite clear. His search must continue and it was just three months later that he was back in Austria this time accompanied by Father Leo Smith, the present Abbot of Buckfast, who was to act as helper and, at times, interpreter.

Chapter 5
In Search

Dom Leo Smith was already familiar with beekeeping as he had often helped in the abbey apiaries during the summer vacations in the mid thirties, finding it a welcome relaxation from his academic studies in Rome. He found the outdoor life a refreshing change from the hours of book work and had enjoyed every aspect of the labour. It was natural therefore that a return to Italy would be most appealing and was to rekindle his interest in bees.

The two monks set off early on a mid-August morning whilst the sun was still a red ball in the grey mist. The year was already showing its age; the balmy short nights of summer had given way to an early morning nip that left the grass beaded with dew and a shimmering silver sea of gossamer transformed the heath of Haldon Moor. Such a good start but now the car radio crackled on and off intermittently. The city of Exeter lay in the valley below, the square towers of the cathedral standing stark in the morning light. It would be well worth a short excursion to the garage as the radio was really needed. Luckily the fault was soon corrected and at last they were on their way following the route to Germany that Brother Adam had taken earlier in the year.

There they stopped at Freiburg University to meet Herr Kaser who had been completing some tests on the resistance that Buckfast bees showed to the disease, acarine. Brother Adam had found the results of this work, which had already been published, very disappointing, but discovered on investigation that the tests had only been conducted in the laboratory where some twenty bees were kept in cages and then infested with the acarine mites. This hardly simulated the effects in a full-size colony which is where Adam had always felt the Buckfast bees' strength lay. He had never claimed his bees were immune to acarine infestation as individuals, but their resistance to it enabled a colony to build up its own strength and so overcome the problem themselves.

The Brother Adam Queen Cage

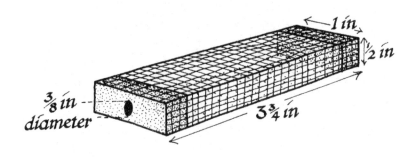

The Brother Adam Queen Cage

From here the couple visited Professor Armbruster at Lindau. Unfortunately they were not expected and the professor had a lecture scheduled for 2pm. However, always the perfect gentleman, sporting his two-piece suit and watch chain, he invited them to join him in a glass of wine and a bite to eat. This allowed just enough time for a discussion on the introduction of queen bees, a subject on which Brother Adam had read a paper at the Leamington Spa Conference in 1950. It had always been accepted that each colony had its own particular odour and that in order to introduce queens successfully it was necessary either to allow the scent of the colony to impregnate the caged queen for a period of time before her release or in some way to mask the varying odours altogether. Adam felt however that this was not the whole story and that the important factor where queens are concerned was to replace like with like with regard to the laying condition so that behaviour patterns and possibly pheromone levels were compatible. Again he feels there is no substitute for practical experience because even though a great deal of research work has been carried out in this subject, it is very different assessing queen acceptance by a nucleus in a laboratory as compared with a honey-production colony in an out-apiary at the cessation of a honey flow. Adam's own comments on introducing queens to such a nucleus are typically colourful: 'Well, yes, you could introduce an elephant and still be all right!'

His own method is simple. The queen and three or four attendant workers are placed in a mesh wire gauze introduction cage of his own making, which is wedged between the top bars of the brood nest. Both ends have a wooden block one of which has a circular entrance hole in it of 3/8 in (9mm) diameter which is plugged with queen candy.

Brother Adam still makes the same soft bee candy that he first prepared under the direction of Brother Columban seventy years ago. The recipe, given in the *British Bee Journal* of September 1905, is followed exactly, even to using the same enamelled saucepan from those early days. The candy consists of white cane sugar, hot water and honey (5oz per 1lb (140g/.45kg) of sugar) and Brother Columban states in his recipe:

> ... to ascertain if it has boiled enough, have a bowl of cold water at hand and firstly dip the fore finger into the cold water, next into the boiling sugar and again into the cold water, and with the sugar that adheres to the finger try to make a soft ball from it like a piece of mastic ready for use!

It takes courage to dip one's finger in the boiling syrup but Adam has no hesitation nor any fear of burning himself. He does say however that it is now impossible to make such smooth candy as in the past as the heat of the gas-ring is nowhere near as fierce as that of the old range they formerly used so the crystals formed are much larger giving a coarser overall texture. If the queen is travelled and so off-lay he may introduce her to a nucleus first or even confine the queen in the cage for 24 hours before replacing the plug with candy, but in any event the queens are released quite happily by the workers eating their way through the candy which takes about 6 hours. So often a valuable queen is rejected or damaged by the workers during introduction and subsequently superceded, but Adam feels this can be easily avoided by taking a little care.

But to return to the journey, each day's travel brought them to another area, another beekeeper, another hive and another bee. Many of the visits had been prearranged and the overnight stops varied from local hotels which were quite inexpensive to the plain hospitality of the village priest or nearby monastery. One beekeeper would contact another and sometimes our pair were sent on a wild goose chase up the narrow mountain passes in the mist and rain. On one such escapade along a mountain pass between Carinthia and Kirkbach, a total of seventy-two hairpin bends had to be negotiated, so that the houses and tall pines that they had passed moments earlier were now dotted about below them as if a part of a child's board game. Fortunately petrol was fairly easy to obtain and no difficulties arose unless the filling station tanks had been serviced by the occupying Russian units. Then the car would cough and splutter as if it had gasped its last until the dirt cleared itself from the carburetor.

High in the Austrian Alps of Carinthia near Klagenfurt Adam found one of the best strains of Carniolan bee. The owner had formerly been head of he

Austrian bank in Graz but had been forced to retire to this remote farm before the war as he would not join the Nazi party. Here at about 12,000ft (3,658m) the fifteen colonies had been preserved in complete isolation. Access to the beehouses had entailed a walk of 1/2 mile (.8km) or more up the mountain track but the effort was well rewarded as the stocks were exceptionally quiet and the downy grey ladies needed no smoke to calm them.

It was already September by the time they reached Italy but the weather was still hot. Crossing the Tyrol they made for Bologna, the centre of Italian bee-breeding. The names here of Caroli, Penna, Aetano Piana (producer of the bright yellow bee) were all familiar. It was the golden bee that had captured the imagination of many beekeepers particularly in North America but it had always showed a marked susceptibility to acarine and Adam felt because of this that its dull cousin, the leather coloured strain from the Ligurian Alps, was far superior.

As they travelled further south the roads became rough and dusty. In the area of Marche, near Ancona there had been a drought for nearly three years at which point the two black monks took on the appearance of millers covered in flour. Their journey through the day had been in convoy and both they and the car were covered in a layer of white dust. At the end of the day they were presented with a bottle of Asti Spumanti to clear their throats; most welcome in the circumstances. In this region of Asti the wine was both plentiful and excellent even if the bees were few. Brother Adam has always taken an interest in wines and as he passed through the different lands never failed to sample those of the region whether they were commercially recognised such as the fruity wines of the Rhinelands or as obscure as the sour vinegar beverage of the Isle of Athos. Secretly perhaps his favourites are the delicate wines from the region of Alsace.

His knowledge of wines may be surpassed by others but not so with mead. He is renowned for both his sack mead - which is sweet and sherry like, maturing for a minimum of seven years in the wood - and also his sparkling mead which is akin to champagne. Even under Brother Columban mead had been made from the washings of the honey cappings, but the methods had been rather inaccurate and the results somewhat variable. Brother Adam had not carried on the tradition and any poor quality honey had been used in the kitchen, often as an ingredient for honey cakes. In 1940 however there was a good crop of heather honey which although of the highest quality had retained a scum and was therefore unsuitable for sale in the jar. Brother Pascal suggested this could be used for making mead and in his usual manner Adam set out to obtain all the information he could on the subject, carefully ascertaining the optimum specific gravity of the liquor with the help of an Austrian chemist who resided at the abbey during the war years.

Then, as now, every ingredient and every stage is prepared with the utmost attention to detail. Water is taken from the pure peaty streams of upland Dartmoor to add to the must and as few chemicals and nutrients as possible are introduced. Only the best quality honeys are used, heather for the sack mead which gives the finished product a deep rich golden hue and a mild clover or lime honey for the sparkling mead. The honey and water are heat sterilised for a few minutes and allowed to cool before a pure culture of Maury wine yeast is added. The sweet type is left to ferment on the lees for a number of years before final maturation in sound oak casks and its eventual presentation on the table after dinner where it will provide an excellent conclusion to a meal. And there is nothing more refreshing after a hard morning's beekeeping than a break for lunch and a glass of the dry sparkling nectar. Preparation for a day's work at the mating station at Sherberton is not complete without a lunchtime bottle quietly cooling in the babbling waters of the Swincombe River.

Our travellers had now reached southern Italy and arrangements had been made to enlist the help of M. Alber on the trip to Sicily as he was familiar with the area. He was a colourful character and proved invaluable as he was a total linguist much travelled in Europe though now resident in Italy. He also had a considerable knowledge of beekeeping and a keen interest in research work, in particular the mating of the honeybee. They began at the foot of the northern slopes of Mount Etna which had erupted just a week before their arrival, but was now all quiet. The state of the colonies in the area was very poor and they contained little brood, for the long hot summer had burned up the flora and little forage would be available until the autumn rains fell. Most of the bees appeared to be hybrids as a result of importations of yellow bees from northern Italy, but Adam did manage to obtain some useful dark queens from the south-east corner of the island.

They returned to the mainland somewhat disappointed. They had planned to visit Sardinia but on the advice of the secretary of the Italian Beekeepers' Association whom they met in Rome they decided to investigate the area of Assisi andá Turin. The day was fine as usual and Father Leo was at the wheel enjoying the coastal scenery when suddenly there was a cry of 'Stop, Stop!' from the passenger seat. Adam had spotted a cluster of Dadant hives nestling in the hillside. Even the car seemed by now to know the order of events and automatically turned in the direction of the apiary as if drawn by a magnet. The effort was well rewarded and several fine queens were obtained.

It was in this way that the trip progressed and it was already October when Father Leo finally had to return to his own commitments and left Adam to visit the important centres of beekeeping research in West Germany. His first call was at the Erlangen Research Institute which unlike the others in Germany favoured the jet-black Nigra bee of the Swiss Alps. He then went on to Marburg, where they were interested in raising a large number of queens in order to help the German beekeepers maintain pure Carniolan stocks. Finally he visited the Celle Institute, just north of Hanover, which supported an island mating station in the North Sea and kept stocks of Italian, Nigra and Carniolans for comparative tests. Adam decided to return to Biberach for a few days subsequent to these visits as he had not been feeling well; the doctor there diagnosed that he was suffering from an attack of shingles. The few days therefore extended into a few weeks and it was Boxing Day before Adam could brave the weather and make a run for home before snow closed the mountain passes. It was a bitter morning when he set off with the temperature well below freezing and an icy wind blowing from the north. He had barely travelled a few miles when the car skidded on a sheet of ice and careered helplessly into a stone pillar. Luckily it was not long before a fellow motorist came by and offered help. Adam had cut his lip badly when his head hit the windscreen, and the front wheels and the radiator of the car had both been so badly damaged that the car had to be towed back to Biberach for repair. Therewas no hope now of Adam reaching England by road before the depths of winter, so in Germany he would have to stay.

It was late February when at last the homeward journey could be attempted. The snow was still very deep over the Schwarzwald and the road ahead shone like a narrow ribbon cutting through the high banks. It would be very easy to slide into one of the drifts and, had that happened, being quite alone, it would have been impossible to extricate himself The warmer lands of France must have been a welcome sight after the hazardous journey, and the vehicle limped safely back to its home garage in Exeter where, unbeknown to Adam, the appearance of the car and the stories of his exploits earned him the name of the 'Mad Monk' from the mechanics.

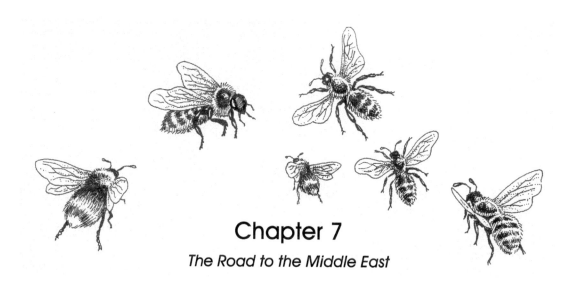

Chapter 7
The Road to the Middle East

The European travels that Brother Adam had undertaken in 1950 took several months and entailed many miles of driving, but the roads were reasonably well maintained and linked centres of civilisation. The journeys he was now to commence in North Africa and the Balkans took him into the realms of the unknown. Not only was the terrain and climate wildly different from our own but so were the cultures and religions.

He left a frozen Buckfast in the depths of winter on 19 February 1952 and by motoring overland across France and then taking a boat trip from Marseilles he stepped ashore a week later amongst the intensely brilliant flowers and the penetrating sunshine of Algiers. He had planned to travel along the coast to Morocco, back to Tunisia and then on to Egypt obtaining visa clearance as he journeyed. His plans were thwarted immediately he arrived in North Africa as the British Embassy informed him that visas would take three or four months and in any event he was advised against entering Tunisia as political unrest had resulted in a revolt. It was the 'Tunisian Bee', so called by Frank Benton in his expedition of 1883, that had initially caught Adam's imagination but he felt all was not lost as its main centre of distribution would most likely be in the high ground of Algeria or 'Tell' as the Arabs called it. His investigations were therefore to be confined to the scrub-lands along the Mediterranean coastal region, the secluded valleys between the snow-capped peaks of the Djurjura mountain range, the plateau wedged between the Atlas mountains and the desert, and a few of the oases that pierced the Sahara itself. It was here in the desert that Brother Adam's endurance was tested to the limit, an ordeal that would never be equalled in the many journeys that were to follow.

The search for perfect specimen queens of the coal black Tellian bee (*Apis mellifera intermissa*) had been very successful and Brother Adam's belief that this was a primary race from which numerous sub varieties, including those of Northern Europe, spread via the Iberian Peninsula, had become stronger. This theory was later confirmed by the biometric studies of Ruttner, so it was only natural that at this time he should be tempted into the arid regions of the Sahara where pockets of totally isolated bees had evolved in the haven of the oases. As Brother Adam set out that March morning, travelling south, the barren landscape had been reborn with the earlier rains and tracts of life adorned by a carpet of brilliant blooms as far as the eye could see. The deceptively mild air was heavy with the sweet scent of nectar and with it awoke the insects that so happily survived on what Adam describes as the 'ephemeral springtime glory'. It was here at the oasis of Laghouat that the most powerful yet good tempered stocks of pure Tellian bees were found, some covering as many as twenty Dadant size combs in March! All hopes of penetrating deeper into the Sahara were dashed when the wind suddenly picked up and an eerie rumbling sound echoed across the shifting sands. The natives said it was Raoul, the invisible drummer that no one had ever seen, and warned of an approaching sandstorm. Greatly disappointed Brother Adam turned north and retraced his route back to Bou-Saada.

His disappointment paled into insignificance when after a few miles travel the full extent of his plight became apparent. The wind now wailed across the desert and with it a dark wall of sand was approaching at speed. Within a few minutes the blazing desert sky became as black as night, the heat was searing in the extreme. The desert track, which had been rough and uneven on the outward journey, was now almost impossible to follow. To add to his discomfort the only way to prevent the car radiator from boiling was to have the interior heat on full. If he were to miss his way there was no water for miles around and his situation would become very desperate. Should he stop or shelter? Well it was too late now. The bizarre rock shapes of mushrooms and pedestals had been formed over the centuries by the blasting of the wind-borne sand, but now on this return journey they seemed more threatening than humorous. Constantly in his head pounded the question 'would the car keep going in such conditions?'. Mile after mile, hour after hour his faith kept him pressing on but imagine his feeling of relief when the vague shapes of habitation loomed through the dusty haze. He had reached civilisation at last, but the terrifying journey has always remained sharp in his memory.

After an exciting and productive month of expeditions he made his way back to Algiers and as he was unable to travel to the Middle East by road, he decided to return to Marseilles and take a passage direct to Israel. The plan was excellent but the voyage was unfortunately dreadful. The vessel was an Israeli one which had been converted from an English collier and the accommodation was extremely poor and overcrowded. The trip had been delayed for 24 hours because of a heavy storm, but though the wind had dropped there was still a big sea running. Brother Adam felt almost intimidated in his Benedictine habit as he was the only Christian on board, and he received a very hostile exchange of words from two of his fellow passengers who accused him of attempting to convert them. In fact one fanatical lady was quite abusive saying, 'You come to pervert us, not convert us!' and so despite a desire to stretch his legs on deck, and suffering from a heavy cold, he decided to keep to his cabin as much as possible.

After a very long seven days he eventually stepped ashore in the relatively new state of Israel, which seemed to him a scented garden full of colourful wild flowers and orange groves. The next morning he visited the Ministry of Agriculture in Tel Aviv where he was introduced to Mr Ardi, the agricultural adviser to the government, who offered to be his guide. The attitude here was reassuringly different to that he had experienced on the boat and Brother Adam was extended every courtesy. He had been offered the hospitality of a community settlement or kibbutz, and as it was the Thursday of Holy Week and they were celebrating Passover, Brother Adam was invited to attend the festivities. It was a great occasion and the various courses of the meal were interspersed with a period of silence followed by a reading from the book of Exodus. Brother Adam was made to feel quite at home with the Jewish community and he felt that he had been accepted for what he was.

The government itself was very forward thinking in many of its agricultural projects, and beekeeping was no exception. Isolated mating stations had been established for the purpose of breeding and supplying queens of a tested pure Italian strain to all beekeepers at the expense of the state. Most of the commercial apiaries were based on the kibbutz system which often ran large-scale operations with 1, 000 or more colonies.

Adam found, as he had expected, no clear differentiation between the bees of Lebanon, Syria and Palestine simply because there were no natural barriers to separate them. Without exception the bees of this area were all irascible, and as soon as the colonies were disturbed an angry hissing mass hotly pursued anyone in the vicinity. However they did need to be defensive as during the dry season it was a struggle for survival with no pollen or nectar sources from July until November and frequent attacks by ferocious hornets and the insidious wax moth. Strange wicker baskets covered in clay, stoneware jars and cylindrical clay pipes, were all part of the beekeeping scene in these Arab states. Such methods had been used for centuries and suited the habitual swarming tendencies of the prolific native bee; but gradually modern commercial methods, large movable-frame hives and more manageable strains of bee have been introduced.

It was not only the bees that Brother Adam found hostile; even after a long hazardous trek across the Syrian desert the customs officials showed the same antagonism. A considerable number of samples, all bottled and carefully labelled for biometric measurements, had been acquired and the border authorities believed Brother Adam planned to sell these for personal profit in the market place at Damascus. There was no point in refuting the allegations or attempting any word of explanation, or the hours already spent waiting at the border check in the sweltering heat would probably turn into days. Wisely he thought it better to pay the duty, albeit excessive, and slowly, deliberately, each phial was carefully scrutinized, fastened with an official seal and replaced into its tray before Brother Adam could finally repack the car.

The Lebanon itself had a higher annual rainfall which supported a luxuriant vegetation making it a beekeeper's paradise. The country displayed a vast range of flora from the miniature wild red clover on the poor soil of the hillsides to the steamy citrus groves of the rich plantations. The native bee was however no asset to this Utopia, quite the reverse in fact, although the stocks to the far north of the country showed a little more promise possibly due to an Anatolian influence.

The culture of these Middle East states contrasted sharply with those of north West Africa. Unlike the women of Tunisia who seemed solely to grace and adorn the household and its social events, the fairer sex here were the labourers whilst the men sat all day drinking coffee and discussing politics. Adam would see them go out early in the mornings to toil all day in the fields, only returning when the shadows began to lengthen laden with huge bundles of kindling on their backs so heavy that 'their noses nearly seemed to touch the ground'. The centuries have changed these lands and their customs but very little. Each evening, as in biblical times, the evening breeze rose at almost exactly 9 o'clock and the women, standing in groups of two and three, would take advantage of it and winnow the corn by tossing it in flat shallow baskets. It was their task too to carry water from the well and the huge heavy clay pots, filled to the brim, would be balanced on their heads on a plaited straw ring and carried gracefully away.

The Island of Cyprus was just a short boat trip from Beirut and Adam was very keen to observe these bees in their native land. At that time this Mediterranean 'Isle of Copper' was a British Crown colony and though the tension between the Greek and Turkish factions was building up, the open hostility between the two groups would not break out for another three years. During modern times it has been too dry for outstanding crops of honey, but Egyptian records from 600BC show that bees have always been part of the life of Cyprus. Interestingly all imports of honeybees had been strictly prohibited and as a result not only did the colonies exhibit outstanding uniformity but no bee disease of any kind was present on the island. Brother Adam had been familiar with the Cyprian strains for over thirty-three years and subsequently was able to confirm his beliefs that the pure stock would over winter better in the Devon climate and develop faster in the spring than any other race. In fact Adam has never lost a colony of this strain over the winter months, which is quite exceptional.

It was early June when Brother Adam began his investigations in Greece itself, discovering the fascinating combination of the skills of an ancient civilisation and those of modern crafts and technology. On the one hand there was a very efficient bee culture that probably comprised more commercial beekeepers than any other country in Europe, and certainly maintained over 700,000 colonies in total. In contrast clay-coated wicker baskets which supported nine movable combs, shaped like wild comb, were still in use as they had been for over 3, 000 years. Perhaps the innovation of the movable-frame hive in America in 1851 was not such a revolutionary idea!

Under the able guidance of the technical adviser to the Greek Ministry of Agriculture, Adam spent three exhausting weeks investigating, it seemed, every corner of every island. This included a trip to Crete though the excursions to some of the other islands in the Aegean had to be postponed because of a shortage of time. According to Greek mythology it was on the rocky isle of Crete that the birth of the bee took place. To Adam's surprise he found that the bees themselves stood apart from those on the mainland particularly in their temper, which left a little to be desired, and also in their lack of uniformity. These findings were confirmed by Professor Ruttner's biometric studies published in 1980 in the German beekeeping journal, *Apidologie*. The Cretan bee was described as a separate geographic race and named *Apis mellifera adami* after the 'explorer' who collected the samples for the studies. This was indeed a great honour and one well deserved.

The heaths and heathers that grow on Crete were yet another fascination for Brother Adam. The mountain thyme, *Thymus capitatus*, that produces the much acclaimed Mount Hymettus honey in the region to the east of Athens, also grows throughout southern Greece and in profusion on Crete. However besides the familiar ground-cover plants, various tall heaths were also in evidence. They also are a feature of the sheltered garden of the home apiary at Buckfast today where a wide collection of heathers from both the genera *Erica* and *Calluna* add all-year-round colour and interest. Studied, selected and planted by Brother Adam with his usual thorough approach, these colourful cultivars, especially the winter heath (*Erica carnea*), also provide an early source of nectar and pollen for the bees.

Subsequent breeding of these Greek strains of bee demonstrated to Brother Adam that the native bee of this area, *Apis mellifera cecropia*, displays a rather drab external appearance but is undoubtedly of great value to beekeeping. It shows less inclination to swarm and greater fecundity than its close relative, the carniolan, and the samples he procured proved well worthwhile. From Greece he had planned to visit Ljubljana in Yugoslavia, travelling via Sarajevo, but unfortunately on his last day in Greece he suffered a puncture which proved beyond repair. Without a spare tyre he opted to take the more travelled route through Zagreb, and from Carniolan country he went on to the Ligurian Alps in northern Italy where he had made a brief visit in October 1950. It had been too late in the year on that occasion to contemplate sending queens back to England, but as this bee had taken pride of place at Buck-fast for thirty-five years or more he knew now exactly what he was looking for.

The search for this tawny coloured bee began in the mountainous region between La Spezia and Genoa and after a few days his efforts had been well rewarded. The queens were carefully packaged and labelled ready to slip in the post to Buckfast next morning, and he could retire to bed well satisfied with his achievements. As is so often the case, pride comes before the fall and he awoke the next morning to find both the packages and the table on which he had left them covered in a mass of tiny black ants trailing to and fro. In panic he tore at the parcels but thousands of the hateful creatures fell out of the cotton wool packing and ran disorientated over his fingers. In all of the twelve cages not one queen nor one of the attendant workers was left alive. This was probably the most disappointing moment throughout these expeditions, as it was impossible to retrace his steps and replace these valuable queens.

It was now seven months since he had left England and though he had hopes of continuing his search his energy and enthusiasm were at a low ebb. He started the long trek home and, finally, by the end of September, he had returned to the familiar rolling hills of Devon. There was much work to be done at Buckfast in the apiaries and the honey crop was also awaiting extraction, but his main task was to make use of the queens he had sent home that summer. Firstly the lines were observed in their pure forms and their characteristics both good and bad assessed in the role of a honey production colony. Then the pure line was crossed with the pure Buckfast strain of the time and the resultant first cross observed in the same manner.

The selection of a breeder queen from a first or second cross is a long and arduous task. Firstly from a batch of newly emerged virgin queens 20 per cent are selected for colour- generally a uniform leather colour being preferred, rather than the extremes of black or yellow - and these queens are then mated under controlled conditions. After twelve months' scrutiny and from a minimum sample of 50 queens the best 3 or 4 are selected and a number of daughters raised from them; the best resultant progeny after a further year's evaluation will be chosen to mother the line. Colour plays no part in selection at this stage and certain lines may be followed for many years only to find they do not come up to expectation and be dropped. Such an example is the Finnish bee for which Brother Adam had high hopes; but after twelve years of promising results the progeny still showed a marked tendency to use propolis and build brace comb, so the line was finally abandoned.

Adam pursues this breeding work not only at Sherberton but by observing all his colonies and selecting the various characteristics he requires at every stage. No written record was kept in the early days but every detail was firmly fixed in his head and he could recall the pedigree of any particular colony. Even today, though careful records are maintained, notes are minimal and on examination of a colony a series of pencilled hieroglyphics are scribbled in a small dog-eared notebook which is then thrust back into the pocket of his black apron. His gift for bees and years of experience enable him to earmark good colonies whilst carrying out routine examinations. The size of a colony and its comparative abilities to store honey indicate longevity, wing power and a zest for work. The appearance of the brood points quickly to the fecundity of the queen and the tendency of the colony to swarm and the general hive cleanliness and hygiene indicates. the resistance of the bees to disease. The general appearance of the super combs will give more information - perhaps an annoying use of propolis and brace comb may be observed. Again, some bees are more inclined to store in the supers whilst others prefer to pack, first pollen and then honey, around the brood area and then fill the outside combs completely with stores before moving above the queen excluder.

The gentleness and behaviour of colonies can vary enormously. In commercial beekeeping it is essential to have a quiet bee that needs little smoke to calm it and which does not shun the light as soon as the crown board is removed. Time can be ill spent searching for a queen, and valuable minutes wasted waiting for a colony to settle before an inspection can commence. It is also important to know how well a colony overwinters and the amount of stores it uses over that period. For this reason all colonies at Buckfast are fed and weighed in the autumn, and weighed again in the spring. The problem is even more complex as first crosses tend to exhibit what is known as hybrid vigour; but this is often associated with a tendency to swarm and be of uncertain temper, characteristics which are often reduced in subsequent generations,

To add to the confusion, reciprocal crosses do not always produce identical characteristics. For example a Buckfast queen mated with Anatolian drones will produce a colony of bad temperament whereas an Anatolian queen mated with Buckfast drones will produce one of quiet and even temper.

Although Brother Adam was anxious to continue his search in other lands the planning of the breeding programme completely occupied him the following year and it was not until early in 1954 that he resumed his quest.

Chapter 8
Onward to Asia Minor and Egypt

The preparations for a journey had become almost routine now. The queen cages, the sample phials, the beekeeping equipment and apparatus all had its correct place. The garage too had become familiar with the necessary adaptations and long list of spares, so that when Brother Adam set out in 1954 all went like clockwork. He picked up the threads where he had left off by passing directly through Greece into the north eastern area of Asia Minor searching for the industrious Anatolian bee of northern Turkey. At this time the road between Istanbul and Ankara was just a dirt track, with many pot-holes and no signposts. Adam followed the major roads, such as they were, checking his direction of travel with a compass and found his whereabouts without too much difficulty. When he returned to this region eight years later he found the track had been transformed into a tarmac motor road which eased the hazards of driving considerably.

On this second visit in 1962 the rivers were still in spate from heavy spring rains making the north and north-east part of the country extremely boggy, and many of the roads were flooded. He therefore confined his searches to the barren land of central Turkey where the summers are hot and dry and the winters intensely cold, which had led to the development of an extremely hardy native bee, the Anatolian.

It was here on the shores of Lake Egridir, in spite of having heavy-duty tyres fitted before he left England, that Brother Adam burst a tyre and the car careered down the bank along the lakeside and somersaulted into a mound of pebbles. The windscreen and quarter-light were smashed and in fact the car appeared a complete write off. It had all seemed to happen so slowly and deliberately as if he were watching it happening to someone else. He was not at all aware of the awful crunching and scraping sounds of metal upon stone, nor the sounds of tinkling glass, in fact he heard no sound at all. Neither did he feel pain, just a sensation of floating towards the inevitable.

How long he lay there he could not tell, perhaps only seconds, maybe minutes or even longer; but eventually he crawled from the wreckage and sat on a boulder on the roadside attempting to stop the flow of blood, from his cut ear, which was trickling down his neck. The injury was not as bad as he first feared and fortunately it was only a few minutes before another vehicle came along with three men in it, who immediately stopped to help. They righted the car and pulled it back up the sloping embankment and miraculously the engine burst into life at the first touch of the starter. Alas the bodywork of the car was badly damaged and the broken windscreen could not be replaced until his return to Salonika in Greece several weeks later where there was an Austin dealer. Many of the samples had burst from their boxes with the force of the impact but at least the car was still operational and he would still be able to return through northern Yugoslavia as he had planned.

This journey of 1962 had been quite extensive, having begun in Morocco in late March where he searched around the area just south of the snow-capped Haut Atlas range in his quest for good specimens of the native bee *Apis mellifera sahariensis*. Since his first journeys he had also made shorter trips similar to the Asia Minor one of 1954, to the Aegean isles in 1956 and the Iberian peninsula in 1959. He was fast becoming a familiar figure in the beekeeping world and in 1958 he had submitted a paper entitled 'The Honeybees of Asia Minor' to the International Beekeepers Congress in Rome. It was here he met P. Haccour, a large commercial beekeeper from Morocco, who was instrumental in executing the well-organised itinerary across the Atlas Mountains via the Col du Zad and thence to the oases that fringed the Sahara. The distinct yellow Saharan race was present only in these Moroccan oases, Figuig being the most easterly and Quarzazate the one furthest to the west in which they were found. The most southerly point their expedition reached was Zagora and the country beyond this Adam describes as 'an endless waste of sand', but just to the north east lay a group of oases, the Tafilalet, which seemed to be the cradle of the aggressive Saharan bee.

This Saharan bee bore little resemblance to any other species of *Apis mellifera* that Adam had studied and indeed his first impression was that it seemed more akin to the Indian bee (*Apis cerana*). Perhaps it had been transported to these isolated areas by the Jewish immigrants thousands of years earlier or maybe as the climate changed and the savannah of the Sahara turned to desert these isolated pockets of surviving vegetation continued to support this hardy little creature. This latter theory is the one Adam supports today as he feels that this race is a relative of the small yellow defensive bee of Central Africa. Interestingly enough this species seems to be the only honeybee Brother Adam has studied that he finds is totally resistant to the fungus disease, chalk brood.

The early summer months are ones to be spent in England working with the bees and Brother Adam always endeavours to meet this aim. The year 1962 was no exception and saw the return from the Middle East for this period. At one time his bees were his love, now they were his life and he followed them from one continent to another and then back to Buckfast to continue the breeding work. Continually comparing, assessing, evaluating, his brain never stopped, never deviated, never faltered. He had no wife or children to distract him, nor thought for food or a roof over his head; he was here to serve and to follow the bees. It was not all just stubborn determination as he is undoubtedly gifted with powers of observation and selection.

He is able to recognise the differences and similarities of his colonies over a period of years whether they are in different hives, different apiaries or even in different continents. A few years ago he produced a Greek cross that exhibited uneven domed cappings that allowed an air space above each cell full of honey, which gave the honeycomb a crusty white appearance. At the end of that season there were a few surplus queens of this line and he gave one of them to a local beekeeper who often visited him at Buckfast. The following season Brother Adam was invited to visit the local Honey Show and untypically, as he had not become involved in the show scene, accepted the invitation. He took a keen interest in the exhibits and his attention was taken immediately by the winner of one of the classes - two sections of comb honey which looked to have very characteristic cappings. Discrete enquiries confirmed that the sections were indeed produced by a colony headed by his Greek queen. How many of us could be so accurate in our comparisons?

It is obvious that the goal for each beekeeper varies enormously and Brother Adam would be the first to tell each apiarist to complete comparative tests on various queens before deciding which strain best suits his needs. Factors of climate, available forage, whether jar or comb honey is to be produced or simply whether pollination is required will all determine the type of bee as well as the hive used and the methods of management. The Buckfast bee has therefore been developed to contend with a constantly damp atmosphere and frequent long periods of rain which may lead to complete crop failure. Until recent years the two crops most likely to give a surplus were white clover (*Trifolium repens*) which generally yields in Devon between mid June and mid July and the ling heather (*Calluna vulgaris*) that secretes nectar from about the middle of August until early September. The Buckfast is a prolific bee, though

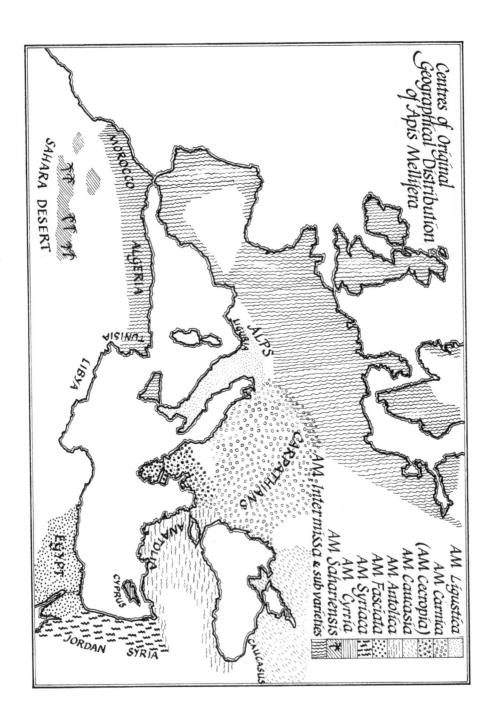

unlike her golden relatives she does not turn every ounce of honey into brood despite the weather conditions or the passing of the summer solstice, so she does need ample area in the brood box to reach her full potential. Perhaps her most immediately noticeable assets, upon examination, are her docility and cleanliness of the boxes together with the lack of propolis and brace comb. Her resistance to disease only becomes apparent after working with her over a period of time.

It was in fact the Egyptian bee that led the field in the least use of propolis, indeed she does not seem to collect it at all. Let us therefore return to October 1962 when Brother Adam flew direct to Cairo and his search for the tiny orange-coloured bee of Egypt was confined to the valley and delta of the Nile and a few of the important oases in the southern section of the Libyan desert. The journeys had now taken on a very different approach as they were well organised in advance and noted scientists and government officials acted as hosts. Adam received a very warm welcome on his visit to Egypt and was much impressed by the enthusiasm and quest for knowledge of the students of the Faculty of Agriculture of Cairo University, who, most afternoons, would take the opportunity of waiting for his return to the hotel so that they could glean every ounce of information possible. To meet this overwhelming demand he gave a series of lectures before his departure, on the more advanced aspects of queen breeding. The Egyptian Ministry of Agriculture was already running several isolated breeding stations in the southern Libyan desert both for pure Italian and Carniolan strains, the latter being most popular with the modern commercial beekeepers. Without a doubt Brother Adam feels that of all the countries he visited, the Egyptians gave him the most enthusiastic welcome, and regular correspondence with his many friends there is still maintained today.

Such an opportunity to visit so many different lands, observing the bees in their native habitat and the different bee cultures, new and old, must surely give one an insight into beekeeping that cannot be acquired from books or study. Brother Adam had travelled some 82,000 miles by road, 7,800 by sea and 7,500 by air in his relentless search for honeybees and when he returned to England in January 1963 at the age of sixty-five he hoped that someone with the necessary facilities and experience would take up the work where he had left off. However he underestimated his own vitality and as he moved into his seventies, he was to make an expedition to the isle of Athos and even more remarkable as he reached his late eighties he was to plan a trip south of the Sahara to the Mount Kilimanjaro region of Kenya and Tanzania .

Chapter 9
The Buckfast Bee

Significant importation of honeybees into Britain began in 1859 with Italian Queens and Buckfast too had been no stranger to such importations since the monastery had been refounded. Brother Colomban had been familiar with Italian, Carniolan and Cyprian strains as well as native British Black bee and as we have seen Adam continued this trend by importing his first pure Cyprianan and Caucasian strains in 1920. He had already realized the potential of different races and crosses both in the resistance to disease, particularly acarine, and in the yields of honey that could be produced. The original Ligurian-Italian Alpine strain that had been crossed with the British Black had been the only ones to withstand the ravages of the Isle of Wight disease and had also shown quite exceptional productivity. He therefore decided that this strain would form the basis of all future breeding programmes.

In 1930 A. W. Gale of Marlborough, Wiltshire, requested that Brother Adam raise 500 queens for him from a very good French bee that he possessed. The season proved a poor one and, as is often the case, in the fickle English weather only 12 out of the 600 virgins that emerged were successfully mated. Disappointingly 10 of these showed susceptibility to acarine, but from the 2 remaining an outstanding cross was produced quite by chance and Adam was so impressed that he incorporated this cross into his own strain some 5 years later. The fifties saw the line breeding, evaluation and subsequent crossbreeding of all the different strains that had been collected on his many travels.

Each year over 500 new queens are produced to overwinter in the nuclei at Sherberton and the best 300 of these are used the following year to head the honey-production colonies. First and foremost in the queen rearing is the preparation of the drone colonies. it being essential that a large number of strong mature drones of 40 days of age after egg lay, are present when the new queens are ready to mate. Thus an approximate schedule of mating periods and emergence times for queens and drones will give the necessary dates for initiating the various manipulations. A minimum of 4 drone colonies headed by sister queens of the required line are stimulated by feeding them a mixture of honey and water and by the addition of combs of sealed worker brood and bees as necessary. Some 6 weeks before the required mating date (i.e. 28 days for the drones to develop and 16 days to mature) one comb, two-thirds of which has been drawn as drone comb. is added to the brood nest in addition to any drone comb the colony may have made of its own accord.

Next the 12 cell-raising colonies are made ready 10 days before the anticipated date of grafting. Strong queenright colonies are chosen with at least 10 frames of brood, and a second brood box with a similar amount of brood is placed above the first over a queen excluder. The colony is therefore extremely strong and the fact that it is overcrowded with 20 frames of brood, and that the queen is separated from the brood in the top box may encourage the bees to draw out queen cells.

Ten days later any queen cells are destroyed and on the morning of the day of the graft, which may be the same day or possibly the following one if the production of the larvae from the breeder colonies has been a little slow, the following manipulation is carried out. The queenless top box which is now filled with sealed brood and any supers, is placed on the site and the queenright lower box removed to one side. Then, having first taken the precaution of finding the queen and ensuring she is retained in the colony that has been moved aside, young bees from some 7 or 8 combs of this latter colony are shaken in front of the queenless box which they will enter. This ensures that the queenless colony has a large amount of sealed brood and a preponderance of young bees and is therefore in a very good position to draw out the queen cells when these are added. The queenright colony with a high proportion of flying bees is then removed to another apiary.

The breeder colonies used to produce the larvae for grafting into the queen cups have to be-prepared 6 days before the anticipated day of the graft. They are first fed 2 quarts (2.2 litres) of dilute honey to stimulate egg production and 2 days later a new warmed comb is placed in the centre of the brood nest. This comb is checked every 12 hours for eggs to note exactly when these are present. Grafting will take place 3 days later, so that the queens are being produced from young larvae less than 18 hours old. Sixty larvae are grafted into pre-warmed wax cell cups carried on 3 carrier bars in a frame, and placed in the centre of the brood nest of the waiting queenless colony which is then fed if there is no apparent nectar flow.

Preparation of the cell building colony

```
┌─────┐
│  B  │   Queenless colony with
│     │   10 frames of brood
├─────┤ Qˣ
│  A  │   Queenright colony with
│     │   10 frames of brood
└─────┘
 SITE A
```

10 days later any queen cells in box B are destroyed

↳ EARLY ON THE DAY OF THE GRAFT

```
┌─────┐
│  B  │   Queenless colony B with young bees shaken from
│     │   7-8 brood combs from A is situated on site A
└─────┘
 SITE A
```

```
      ┌─────┐
      │  A  │   Depleted queenright colony A taken right
      │     │   away to another apiary (Site B)
      └─────┘
       SITE B
```

1-2 hours later — Grafted cell cups are introduced and feed given as necessary

The cell cups themselves are primed with a little royal jelly diluted with sterile water which is sufficient to aid the transference of the larvae. The grafting tool is sterilised with boiling water between each graft to reduce the risk of infection and as soon as each frame has been grafted it is immediately introduced to the waiting colony so that the chance of chilling or dehydration of the larvae is kept to a minimum. Results from the abbey using this method are unusually good and sometimes the acceptance level is as high as 90 per cent but this will obviously vary with each graft and the experience and skill of the technician.

When crossbreeding two distinct races, Adam selects by colour and appearance 520 virgins from 2,000 or so that emerge in the incubator, choosing leather coloured ones rather than the extremes of black or yellow. But in all other cases he prefers not to use the incubator as he feels that for those few hours when a virgin has emerged, it is important that her attendant workers are at hand. He therefore considers totally naturally reared and mated queens to be far superior, and for this reason he distributes the ripe queen cells to the queenless nuclei the day before they are due to emerge.

These nuclei at the isolated mating station consist of 120 Dadant nucleus hives, each divided into 4, with a separate entrance and 4 half-size Dadant frames but with a common tray feeder; and 30 British Standard nucleus hives which accommodate 4 nuclei in a line consisting of half-size British Standard combs. During the season any patches of drone brood, generally minimal in nuclei, are meticulously destroyed so that only the chosen male line from the drone colonies is in evidence. A week before the ripe queen cells are due to be distributed, the nuclei are dequeened and these queens are used to requeen the honey-production stocks. Such a spell of queenlessness greatly increases the acceptance of the queen cells, but any emergency queen cells are destroyed just prior to the introduction. One day before the virgins are due to emerge, the cells are gently suspended unprotected between the brood of the nuclei and then left quite alone for one month by which time the queens will have emerged, mated and come into lay.

These queens remain at Sherberton over the cold wet winter period to assess their over-wintering abilities before being introduced to head a honey-production colony in the following spring. Adam has written many papers, articles and books in support of his breeding work and this has inevitably brought a demand for the bee. Apart from the occasional tested breeder queen, Buckfast stopped the sale of queens in 1937 as the demand had been too great. Gale of Marlborough, as Adam always refers to him had partially filled the gap by selling queens of Buckfast strain, though mated at random. In the late sixties, though, the commercial way forward became clear.

> # BUCKFAST QUEENS
>
> BUCKFAST LEATHER-COLOURED ITALIANS ARE INCOMPARABLE HONEY GATHERERS, EXCEPTIONALLY DOCILE, WONDERFULLY PROLIFIC, AND ALMOST IMMUNE TO DISEASE
>
> BUCKFAST BEES HOLD THE RECORD OF COLLECTING THE LARGEST QUANTITY OF HONEY IN THE SHORTEST SPACE OF TIME, NAMELY, A TOTAL OF NO LESS THAN 135 POUNDS OF SURPLUS WITHIN FIVE DAYS
>
> **Select Fertile Queens 10/6, throughout the Season**
>
> ALL QUEENS SUPPLIED BY RETURN OF POST
>
> **Br. ADAM, The Abbey, Buckfast, Devon**

An advertisement for Buckfast Queens from the *British Bee Journal Beekeepers' Adviser*, August 1929

Adam had the necessary breeder queens but it was not economically viable to produce large quantities of queens in the short unsettled English summer. He had visited Israel in 1965 at the invitation of their bee breeders' association and felt that it would be an ideal centre for such a project. At the time there were ten producers of queens in that country but not all of them met the high standard that Adam required. A meeting was arranged in 1968 with all the queen producers and Mr D. Ardi, Israel's minister for beekeeping, and it was decided that Mr Nathan Merin would be solely responsible for producing the Buckfast queens to be sold in Great Britain. His maximum production would limit the number of queens to 1,500 per annum, which would be distributed through Birdwood Apiaries near Wells in Somerset, England. It was about this time in the sixties that Brother Adam was also corresponding with Roy Weaver of Weaver Apiairies, Navasota Texas, who are still one of the largest producers of queens and package bees in the world. When they met in person at the Apimondia Congress at College Park, Maryland, in 1967 the question arose concerning the production of Buckfast queens in North America. It was agreed that breeding stock would be obtained through their mutual friends Dr. G. Townsend and Dr. V. M. Smith of the Ontario Agricultural College in Canada, as direct imports of queens from Great Britain had not been allowed since the twenties. Similar to the agreement with Israel, Weaver Apiaries would be the sole producer of Buckfast Bees in North America in return for a Royalty on every Queen ever sold.

Initially the majority of purchases were by hobby beekeepers as the royalties resulted in rather a high price compared with other queens. Subsequently tests carried out by the university of Minnesota in 1979 and 1980 on commercially available queens showed the Buckfast to be superior and sales boomed. The arrival of the acarine mite in North America in 1984 has made the resistant Buckfast bee more popular than ever and sales now exceed that of any other strain produced by Weaver Apiaries. It is hoped that with the cooperation of the US Government, new imports of breeding material will enable a broader based programme to take place, as it has been difficult to maintain comprehensive stocks with limited imports of semen from the drones of the breeding colonies in Devon.

The appearance of the varroa mite, too, has altered the course of beekeeping and in an attempt to keep the pest out of Britain all importations of bees from Israel and other infested areas have been suspended. Consequentially the production of Buckfast queens for the British market now takes place in North America. Brother Adam did not wish to become personally involved in the commercial aspects of the sale of queens so at first this was handled by the Birdwood Apiaries as previously mentioned, but was eventually taken on by Dr .F. Corr.

John Corr first met Adam in 1960 when he and a friend, both beekeepers, travelled from near Belfast in Northern Ireland to spend a week at the abbey in return for a week assisting with the bees. The days flew by and the two Irishmen enjoyed the working break so much that the visits were repeated. Dr Corr and Brother Adam soon became firm friends and an invitation to visit Northern Ireland was accepted and has now become an almost annual event. The distribution problems that had arisen with the queens were naturally discussed and Dr Corr, having considered the matter carefully, offered to take over this responsibility which would come as a welcome contrast to his hospital work in mental health. Adam too was relieved by this decision as he felt he could trust Dr Corr to put the wellbeing of the queens and the interests both of the abbey and the purchasers foremost. The operation ran quite smoothly even in troubled Belfast, though recent months have seen more complex arrangements brought in by the authorities over the import licences.

A similar course of events soon followed in Germany. Herr Fehrenbach was, and indeed still is, the manager of a large fruit growing co-operative in southern Germany. He was also seriously interested in honeybees on a semi-commercial scale. In 1960, in the September issue of the German bee journal, he read the article by Brother Adam which formed the basis of his book, 'Bee-keeping at Buckfast Abbey'. He was so impressed that he immediately wrote to Adam and eventually arranged to meet him at Christmas a year later when Adam was staying with his cousin Maria in Biberach. He was an extremely practical man and had kept bees, mainly Carniolan strains, for many years, but the simple Buckfast methods and logical approach greatly appealed to him.

It was only a matter of time before these methods were incorporated into his own system, the modified Dadant hive playing an important part in the reorganisation. A mating station was set up high in the Alps and Brother Adam supplies all the necessary breeding stock in return for the royalties on the sale of the queens. This system of management in Germany is a little different to the other queen producers in that only 100 or so breeder queens are offered for sale each year, having been tested for a full season. This corresponds with the autumn requeening when the honey-production colonies are dequeened and then united with a mating nucleus. This produces a very strong stock headed by a young queen which will overwinter well in the cold of southern Germany and explode in the spring in order to take advantage of the early winter-sown rape crop. Needless to say the whole Fehrenbach family have become good friends of Brother Adam, and Herr Fehrenbach himself has become an integral part of Adam's team in the more recent journeys.

The demand for Buckfast queens spread throughout Europe and mating stations for the Buckfast strain sprang up far and wide. In the north, breeding stock was supplied to Sweden in return for royalties paid on each queen and the Buckfast Breeders Association, in conjunction with the National Association and the Swedish Government maintain an island mating station for this purpose. Such stations were likewise set up in Luxembourg and France and indeed more recently off the Atlantic coast of France an island mating station was set up, maintained with dronebreeding stock, where virgin queens may be mated in return for a fee. Not only has Brother Adam broken new ground in the assessment of different races of bee and of bee breeding, but he has been commercially successful on behalf of the abbey throughout the world. It was just reward therefore that his efforts should be recognized in the Queen's Birthday Honours list of 1974. Adam was amazed to receive a letter from 10 Downing Street stating that he had been nominated for the *OBE* by the Ministry of Agriculture for 'his services to beekeeping' and his immediate reaction was to ask Abbot Placid if he could accept the honour. The abbot gave his blessing and finally the momentous day dawned when he had to travel to London to receive it. The presentation took place in the magnificent ballroom at Buckingham Palace and his cousin Maria had excitedly accepted the invitation to accompany him. The proud recipients filed in to the soft strains of a string orchestra quietly playing in the background and one by one each name was announced. Adam stepped forward and the Queen pinned the badge on his lapel and exchanged a few brief words on how long he had been keeping bees. It was a far cry from the humble beginnings in Germany and his secluded life in the monastery in south Devon.

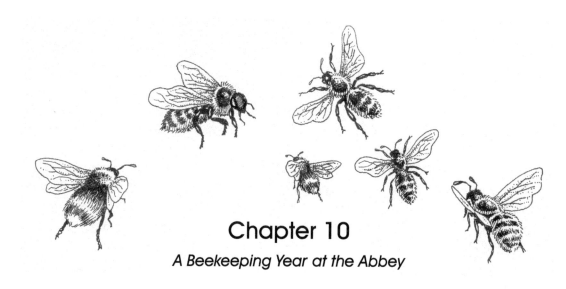

Chapter 10
A Beekeeping Year at the Abbey

We have touched on various aspects of the basic beekeeping at Buckfast such as feeding and extraction, but Brother Adam follows a strict routine during the 'beekeeping year' based on the principles and techniques he has evolved by trial and error over the years from a knowledge of the bees, their habits and idiosyncracies, from mistakes and mishaps together with brilliant forward planning.

As every beekeeper knows, when once the honey crop is removed the procedures that follow are really the start of the next season's beekeeping. The feeding and pre-winter care will determine the strength of the colony that will explode in the following spring. In a good year the majority of the 300 honey producing colonies at Buckfast will come back from the heather minus their supers no later than 10 September. They return to their permanent apiary sites where Brother Adam has endeavoured to provide the ideal situation of southerly aspect and shelter from the prevailing wind, using natural windbreaks to protect the hives; though care has been taken not to reduce the air circulation and create pockets of damp or frost. In any commercial situation easy access is of prime importance and, where necessary, hardcore has been laid on the sites so that vehicles can be brought as close to the hive stands as possible, keeping physical carrying of the hives and heavy equipment to a minimum.

Brother Adam had originally put the hive stands on concrete blocks, but this had necessitated an annual check of the levels as the ground settled. So in 1934 he decided to cast 184 concrete platforms in quick-drying cement each of which would take a wooden hive stand. The stands incorporate a wooden tray into which the boxes fit exactly so that two hives 8in (20cm) apart can be supported without fear of their slipping when the heavy supers are removed. Each leg of the stand consists of a metal pin that locates into a well in the concrete plinth, which again increases stability and allows for an easy height for working the brood box. Although very heavy, the plinths are easily transportable to the out-apiaries and have stood the test of time exceptionally well, only having to be checked every ten years or so.

All the colonies are fed 1 gal (4.5 litres) of 2:1 cane-sugar solution on the eve of their return from the heather so that the central combs next to the shrinking broodnest will be filled with sugar syrup for winter stores. This reduces the risk of dysentery developing as tends to happen when the bees are overwintered on the residue of the heather crop. The colonies are then weighed and any on the light side are given extra feed. If the heather crop has failed, as is often the case if the wind shifts to the cold, drying north-east quarter, the colonies return short of food, with very little brood and generally in poor heart. Under these circumstances Adam feels that a large amount of syrup will overwork and exhaust the autumn bees who then may not last the winter, so he is careful to feed the minimum amount to keep the bees alive until spring, feeding again when the new year's replacement bees have begun to emerge.

The colonies are not fully inspected at this time of year as robbing is always present in some form; but any obviously queenless stocks are requeened and the majority overwintered on ten deep Dadant combs. In south Devon the enemy against successful overwintering is damp, and Brother Adam inserts a strip of wood 1/8in (3mm) thick between the brood body and a crown board to give a little extra ventilation without causing a draught. In the early years he experimented with insulated packing cases, but although the bees came through the winter very strong they failed to build up in the spring, almost as if a spell of severe cold is beneficial and encourages the population explosion in the new year.

The bees are left quite alone, well secured on their hive stands with wires, from October until February when the floor boards are exchanged for a clean set, apiary by apiary. The bees themselves are not disturbed at this stage but Adam does allow a cursory examination of the colonies and frees the entrances of any debris and dead bees. In March the colonies are weighed to assess the consumption of winter stores and are reduced to the number of combs that the bees are actually covering. This serves to condense the broodnest and so keep up the temperature, encouraging the queen to lay. After mid March, once the weather is warm enough, the colonies are equalised so that each covers approximately seven of the modified Dadant combs. This serves to boost the weaker ones and reduce the incidence of swarming later in the year from the stronger colonies. It also makes for easier management as all the colonies in one apiary will require much the same treatment at the same time. It is of course, necessary to have more than one apiary for this method to be successful because if the manipulation were to be carried out on hives within the same apiary, the flying bees covering the brood would return to their original site at a time of year when the deserted brood would be readily chilled and thus lost.

Conveniently, at this time, two-thirds of the colonies are also requeened with the tested overwintered queens from the mating station. Such young queens are generally reckoned to be at their peak in the year after their emergence and will add zest to the expanding colonies whilst again reducing the incidence of swarming. The old queens are returned to the mating nuclei where they will remain until late May when the queen cells are distributed and they are finally pinched out. No difficulties are experienced with this operation as the queens are readily accepted in the spring, and the colonies are small which makes the finding of the old queens quite easy. Similarly no problems seem to arise with the addition of bees and brood to a strange colony, as the colonies are subdued by exposure to daylight for a few minutes prior to transference of the bees which also seem to be quietened by travelling.

Mid April sees the first significant expansion of the stocks and every 10 days another comb is added to the outside edge of the brood cluster. Brother Adam very much respects the sanctity of the broodnest and feels that generally the bees are more aware of their own needs than is the beekeeper. For this reason he does not favour the spreading of brood, or the removal of pollen-clogged combs or needless examinations, and uses the minimum of smoke during his inspections.

Swarm preventative methods with Buckfast bees are generally unnecessary when using young queens, but routine inspections are carried out every 10 days in the swarming season. If a colony seems determined to swarm even after the destruction of all queen cells, the colony is dequeened for a period of some 7 to 10 days, all further queens cells destroyed and then requeened with a young queen. At Buckfast all queens are clipped, a young queen. At Buckfast all queens are clipped, which is helpful for identification, but also in the event of a swarm the queens will fall to the ground and be lost but the bees and their supplies of honey will return to the hive until the first virgin emerges, which allows the beekeeper 'a few extra days' grace.

Supers are added to the colonies when the brood is covering nine combs, which is generally about the third week in May, except when there is an early rape crop. They are added on top of the existing boxes as this encourages the bees to fill and seal the combs next to the brood box particularly late in the year. A full Dadant super weighs about 50lb (23kg) so physical strength is another necessary attribute for working with these hives.

Managing stocks for heather honey is an entirely different game. The achievement of a surplus is somewhat of a gamble. One may reap a good harvest if close, sultry windless days prevail, perhaps achieving more rapid gains than on any other crop, but on the other hand failure may lead to the ruination of good colonies. Secondly the colonies need to be selected and prepared; strong colonies with young queens being needed at a time when the climax has passed and the natural drop in brood rearing ensues. The ling flowers from about mid August until early September so that the trek usually begins with all the honey production colonies around 28 July on average depending on the appearance of the heather. The system of management together with the qualities of the Buckfast bee ensure that if the weather is good a surplus is assured. It is generally reckoned that the heather plant has some twenty years of useful life before it becomes woody and no longer exhibits the young shoots that produce the flowers. Recent years have been disappointing as subtle changes in climate, the minimum of management and overgrazing of the moor as a whole have seen the gradual disappearance of the familiar purple autumn tinge.

Many beekeepers participate in this autumn pilgrimage but after several years Brother Adam finds they fail to appear only to be replaced by newcomers. Few people have the invaluable experience of sixty-seven seasons of attempting to catch a nectar flow which, albeit very intense, is also fickle and short lived. Early in September the hives return from the moor and the year's work is complete. Hopefully the extraction will see the honey tanks full with just the bottling to follow.

One might imagine that as his years passed the three score years and ten mark, retirement would be just around the corner, but not so Brother Adam. Each day begins at 4am unless he has some pressing correspondence and then he rises earlier by an hour or two! After prayer, the daily work starts at 6 and finishes at 4 or 5 pm, with a short break for lunch, and he retires to bed in the early evening after a light meal. Even today in the biting wind it is not unusual to hear the clanking of a bucket as, on hands and knees, he scrubs out the queen-rearing house in preparation for the coming season.

In strict rotation, over a four-year cycle and under his personal supervision, the hive bodies and frames are boiled in caustic soda to keep disease to a minimum. A steel-wire cage, suspended from the ceiling by a pulley arrangement, containing as many as two brood boxes of frames, is slowly lowered into the steaming brew. This removes the paint, wax propolis and any other debris so that the bare wood is then ready for treatment, the hive bodies are emulsioned in 'broken white' which has proved to be the most satisfactory modern protective coating, creoscote being washed out too easily and oil-based paints tending to lift with condensation created by the bees within. The floorboards are treated with Cuprinol to reduce fungal growth but are well aired before use otherwise robbing may be induced. Their external faces are painted the familiar salmon colour to match the roofs.

This cheerful colour scheme was first adopted by Brother Gabriel, a signwriter by profession, in a sign he made for the bee department, and the apiary colour scheme followed suit. He helped Adam with the bees for a number of years in the twenties and thirties but is best remembered for the lovely pastel-shaded designs on the wax paper honey pots and the comb-honey cartons. Alas sections are no longer economic and neither are the seven colour-print waxed-paper cartons. These were obtainable at £7.50 per 1,000 in the mid-twenties and fifty years later when the last batch was purchased the cost was £300 per 1,000. Today that cost would be nearly double, so inevitably they have been replaced by red and white plastic 1lb (454g) containers.

Wax cups for the queen rearing are dipped, introduction cages made by hand, frames and foundation assembled, gates painted, sheds repaired; all winter jobs that are never let slip. The summer months, as we have seen, involves the routine inspections of 300 honey-producing colonies and the main mid-season task of the raising and selection of some 500 queens for the nuclei at Sherberton. Often visiting beekeepers from far-off lands come and stay at the abbey and are happy to give their services for the privilege of working with Adam and the opportunity to discuss the many and varied aspects of beekeeping. Brother Adam is also fortunate in having as his helper at Buckfast, Peter Donovan, who endeavours to reach the high standards of practical beekeeping that are set by the master.

Soon after the beginning of the war, children from the industrial cities were evacuated from their homes and sent to the country because of the incessant bombing raids. Peter was one of a number of children from Gravesend, Kent, that were sent to Buck-fast where he was deposited at the local bus terminus. The children stood awaiting selection by the host families, each clearly labelled and carrying a canvas bag containing a gas mask, a tin of bully beef, one tin of sweets, one orange, a toothbrush and paste and valuable food coupons. When once settled in Devon he attended school, but in his spare time helped out at the abbey apiaries. He was more than anxious to work with the bees full time and when the opportunity arose he lied about his age, left school, and joined Adam when he was only 13 1/2 years old. During this period Adam sent regular reports to his mother informing him of his progress and wellbeing. Three and a half years later in 1945 he was conscripted into the army, in spite of Brother Adam's plea to the authorities that beekeeping was a reserved occupation.

During his army years in the Far East and subsequently when he returned to the East Coast of England he always kept in touch with Brother Adam, often visiting Buckfast on holiday.

As soon as the opportunity presented itself in 1972 to return to Devon he did so and joined Adam once more in the capacity of assistant beekeeper. Essentially a practical man he is very much responsible for the smooth running of the Bee Department under Adam's watchful eye.

The Bee Department at Buckfast is run strictly as a commercial enterprise but it is very apparent that certain aspects of its very existence set it apart from all other beekeeping businesses. Few managers can give their life to their work without thought of house or family as has Brother Adam. Perhaps, too, in other situations the working visitor would not be so readily available and would certainly entail extra overhead costs to the enterprise. Even the abbey itself provides a unique market for the sale of the finished product as many thousands of visitors each year are attracted to this peaceful corner of south Devon to view the magnificent buildings, the stained glass works of the abbey, or taste the famous tonic wine. Indeed the home apiary must surely be the most beautiful 'bee yard' in Britain with its immaculate lawns and neat flower-beds set against the backcloth of sweeping beeches that overhang the swift-flowing river Dart.

Chapter 11
Modern Methods

Brother Adam has always stressed the practical aspects of his work and indeed in beekeeping as a whole, but it would be wrong to assume that his interest did not encompass any scientific work that would have useful applications. The instrumental insemination of queen honeybees is just such a subject. The technique had first been successfully developed by L. R. Watson in the late 1920s, but Adam did not appreciate the application to his own work until just after the war. He had read with keen interest the progress in this field by Harry Laidlaw, Otto Mackensen and W. C. Roberts of the Bee Breeding and Stock Centre at Baton Rouge, Lousiana, USA.

Dr Roberts was also involved at this time with the controversy over the possible existence of multiple matings, having noted that more than half the virgin queens returned to the mating nucleus on more than one occasion with a mating sign. It was assumed that on these occasions the queen was improperly mated and so had taken a second mating flight, there being no suggestion up to this time of routine multiple matings. V. V. Triasko, well known for his later research in this field in Eastern Europe put forward the suggestion in 1951 that the queen mates with several drones, perhaps 4 or even 5 on one flight, but it was not until 1953 that the position was clarified by Professor F. Ruttner in his experiments on the volcanic island of Sicily in the Mediterranean. He demonstrated that after the first mating flight a queen contained more semen than could be produced by one drone and that out of 140 queens observed, over half exhibited a mating sign more than once. It was therefore concluded that each queen mates naturally with several drones, perhaps 9 or 10, and that the semen is stored in clumps in the spermatheca. Brother Adam considers this fact to be of prime importance and one that has great application to his breeding programme, increasing variability and reducing inbreeding. Indeed he says it is the most important factor to be understood since Father Dzierzon expressed his belief in parthenogenesis in 1835.

There was a good opportunity for Adam to discuss such matters at the Annual Beekeepers Congress of Apimondia, and it was in this way in 1948 that he first became personally acquainted with Dr Roberts. They met at many subsequent gatherings and indeed in 1965, after they had attended the Congress in Bucharest, Dr Roberts and Dr Townsend of the University of Toronto accompanied Adam on a journey to Istanbul and northern Greece.

Adam had obtained a full-field dissecting microscope suitable for instrumental insemination in 1949 and Dr Roberts subsequently presented him with the necessary apparatus which was the first of its kind in Britain. Dr Butler and Dr Simpson of the Rothamsted Experimental Institute had visited the United States to receive tuition in the necessary skills for this technique some two years earlier and therefore visited Buckfast in connection with this work. The results were somewhat disappointing; they attempted to inseminate each queen on two separate occasions so that a high level of semen would be instilled, but the risk of infection was doubled. Without the use of antibiotics as a prophylactic, and with the somewhat unsophisticated equipment adding to the difficulties caused by lack of practice, the loss of queens was inevitably high. In spite of these adversities however the attempts at insemination continued, but it was not until the mid seventies that the process became much more successful. Brother Adam had been visiting the home of Professor Kirn of the Medical Faculty of the Bosch University in Stuttgart who had developed, in conjunction with a brilliant technician, Herr Joseph Haidinger, an extremely accurate and well-designed inseminating apparatus.

Adam was immediately impressed with the instrumentation. The microscope gave a much larger field of view and a cold light had been incorporated to give better illumination without the problems of increased heat. The probes themselves were controlled by a screw in both the vertical and horizontal planes, giving a wider angle of approach which enabled the operator to have greater precision and easier manipulation of the valve fold. Much to Brother Adam's delight a duplicate apparatus was later given to him in celebration of his birthday. Haidinger is extremely skilled in this technique and nowadays during his summer vacations travels throughout Germany providing a queen-insemination service for local beekeepers. He has often visited Buckfast and his patience in helping the beekeeping staff at the abbey to perfect the operation has proved invaluable.

Beekeepers in England often express the view that instrumental insemination is of purely academic interest, or at least an expensive challenge for the eccentric, but Brother Adam has shown that there is a valid use apart from in the laboratory. He is able to maintain several pure strains of differing lines without setting up separate mating stations, so that his breeding programme is now far more controllable. There is also the possibility of sending semen across the Atlantic so that a new injection of the Buckfast strain can be made at will.

During the seventies Brother Adam was more than pleased with the achievements he had made with the Buckfast strain and as we have seen he had investigated every conceivable strain of honeybee and, where appropriate, incorporated it into his own. He had always been impressed with the Greek bee but during his travels he was concerned that it always appeared to lack uniformity. Even centuries ago Aristotle had distinguished between a yellow and a black variety of honeybee and had noted a difference in their temperaments. What was needed was an isolated pocket or an island where no migratory beekeeping had been allowed, nor any importations made. The isle of Athos was just such a place and quite by chance Brother Adam had been given a descriptive book of the island by a keen German beekeeper who had also visited Buckfast. The island was under the control of the Greek Orthodox Church and supported twelve main monasteries and a number of hermits who lived on the rocky hillsides. No casual visitors or settlers were permitted to land, nor indeed the female of any species. Its isolation was therefore complete and an obvious choice as the monks themselves tended a few stocks of bees.

The wheels were set in motion to make such a visit possible. Extracts from Brother Adam's books had already been published in the Greek journal of apiculture so that obtaining the support of the Greek Ministry of Agriculture presented little difficulty. Permission had also to be obtained from the patriarch in Istanbul who was head of the Orthodox Church and, when the military governor of Athos also gave his consent, the date for the trip was set. The party settled down in a lovely hotel on the mainland and awaited the decision of the civil governor. At first a delay of two weeks was proposed as the objection was raised that too many applications for visits had been made in recent months. With some persuasion and the fact that the other three letters of consent had already been granted, the permit was finally issued. The local police had then to be informed of the intentions and the final clearance was made. BBC Television wished to record the expedition but it was feared that the necessary permits from the parliament of monks to allow them to film might be witheld. However at the last minute a telegram of approval arrived.

The party, consisting of Brother Adam, Mr Vld. Dermatopoulos who would act as guide and interpreter, Dr Corr from Northern Ireland, Herr Fehrenbach from Germany, Mr Colin Weightman from the north of England and the television crew, set off by boat early one August morning in 1981. When they arrived at the tiny port they were met by customs officials who immediately attempted to confiscate all cameras, but luckily their permits held them in good stead and they were allowed to proceed by bus, along the only road on the island, to the parliament. Visiting police from the mainland were employed here and they checked and verified all the credentials. Then finally the parliament of monks, which was controlled by representatives of all twelve monasteries, removed the last obstacle.

It was already past 11:00am and the party agreed to take lunch before proceeding any further. Brother Adam describes the hotel and restaurant as being 'primitive in the extreme, the food being less than basic'. Soup, vegetable only, was served with good bread and followed by oranges accompanied by a sour wine. The beds, four to a room, consisted of bare boards and a blanket.

The following day the television crew made arrangements to hire a bus and visit a hermitage in the east of the island where two monks kept some stocks of bees. Unfortunately, on their arrival, they found the beekeeper of the two was missing so even though Brother Adam was able to examine the colonies, it was not possible to select any queens. He left the queen cages with the other monk and was delighted to be met on his departure from the island with a gift of queens, honey and coffee, all from the absent beekeeper.

An attempt at making a garden had been tried around the main monastery and a few vegetables fought for their existence in the poor dusty soil. The countryside beyond was wild primitive forest which reflected an earlier era when this part of the Mediterranean had a high rainfall and supported a luxuriant vegetation. The monks themselves survived by leasing sufficient of the timber woods to cover the cost of their meagre fare, purchasing such items as oranges, dried peas, coffee and very sweet walnuts preserved in sugar. Meals, such as they were, were accompanied by a very sour wine, akin to vinegar, so that although the monks were most hospitable, monastic life was very basic. In fact everything was basic in the extreme, except the library which was something of an enigma in this primitive way of life. Dating back over a thousand years, it contained many hundreds of rare and valuable books.

Apart from the television programme which was of interest to the general public, the trip was also a success with regard to the breeding material obtained. These Athos queens brought back from the expedition have proved to be very productive here in England and Brother Adam is continuing to use them for crossbreeding with regard to his own strain.

Gradually the word 'Buckfast' has become familiar to every beekeeper in Europe and indeed throughout the world. Lectures and symposia on Brother Adam's work in French, German, English and Swedish have become commonplace. Recognition has followed. His native country honoured him in 1975 with the Verdienstkreuz, which is the German equivalent of being included in our own Honours List. The presentation was made at a reception at the German Embassy in London, followed by a traditional luncheon. The Central Swedish Beekeepers Association also bestowed a Gold Medal upon him in 1970 in honour of his achievements and made him an honorary member of their association. He was also nominated for an honorary doctorate from the Faculty of Agriculture of Uppsala University in Sweden, which was presented in October 1987.

The yearly toil amongst the apiaries of Buckfast continued, as it does today, unchanged, but Adam did not even then feel his work was over. His evaluation of honeybee races must now take him south of the Sahara to the regions of Mount Kilimanjaro and Mount Kenya in East Africa. It was the placid races *Apis mellifera monticola* in particular, the large dark bee to be found in the rain forests of these mountainous areas - that were of most interest although the vitality of the smaller yellow races also warranted investigation. Some work had already been done by Professor M.V. Smith of Canada (1961) and Professor F. Ruttner (1975 and 1984) on the biometric measurements and the relative locations of these races but no mention had been made of their behavioural patterns, apart from defence, or their likely commercial potential either as a pure race or in crossbreeding.

The African races of honeybee exhibit many characteristics that bear no relation to the European strains, but their vitality and ability to survive under harsh conditions is enormous. It was these qualities that tempted Brother Adam to investigate this continent further as he felt sure that by breeding he would be able to control the problems of extreme defence, of inherent swarming and absconding, and nervousness on the combs.

For the Love of Bees

Chapter 12
Into The Eighties

It was during the September following Brother Adam's eighty-ninth birthday that the expedition to the south of the Sahara began. The rain forest areas of Mount Kilimanjaro in Tanzania and of Mount Kenya had been chosen as being of most interest, for it was here that the so-called black bee of Africa, *Apis mellifera monticola*, was said to be found. As already mentioned, Professor Smith in the early sixties and Professor Ruttner in the mid-eighties had visited these areas and carried out biometric studies of the indigenous honeybee races. It had been reported that this bee did not exhibit the aggression of the smaller yellow African races, and also could survive at fairly high altitudes where the temperatures would plummet from the high 70s F (20s C) during the day to almost freezing at night.

Brother Adam was to be accompanied by his friend Herr Fehrenbach from southern Germany and daughter Rosalind, whose services as a medical doctor would be invaluable; Michael van der See from Holland who is an avid supporter of the work of Buckfast; Walter Davie, a bee diseases officer with the Ministry of Agriculture in Great Britain and myself. It also happened that at this time York Films, in the shape of Mr & Mrs David Taylor and a film crew, were documenting the life and work of Brother Adam for a television programme and so were able to make a film record of the trip.

It had been arranged that we should all meet on the evening of September at Arusha in Tanzania, which lies at the south western foot of Mount Kilimanjaro. The German contingent, Brother Adam and the film crew were flying direct to Dar es Salaam and thence by air to Kilimanjaro Airport, while the rest of us were to join forces in Nairobi, Kenya, one day later and cross the border by road. Relationships between the two countries have been somewhat strained in recent years and indeed the border had been completely closed for a time.

This restriction had been relaxed latterly although it was still not permissible to take a hire car from one country to the other.

Being the last of the party to arrive in Kenya just before dawn, we were swiftly escorted to a waiting vehicle and were soon speeding into the harsh morning light. Straggling giraffes galloped out of the way of the oncoming vehicle, soon to become distant specks in the never ending red dusty savannah. Strange orange castles intricately fashioned by their resident termites towered between the scrubby acacias which were just bare silver thorns because of the lack of rain. Brightly clad Masai natives in scarlet tartan cloth loped across the plains in pairs, each carrying a stick as a sign of their masculinity and prowess as a herdsman. It was still only breakfast time when we reached the border and began filling the inevitable forms in triplicate for the customs and passport control.

We found ourselves in a dusty border town amid a colourful tribal people who persistently tried to sell us their wares. It was much earlier than our original estimated time of arrival and so, unconcerned, we waited patiently for sight of the prearranged transport which was to be sent to meet us on the Tanzanian side of the border. Lunch hour approached and by courtesy of the Kenyan customs office we were able to ascertain that a vehicle had left Arusha, though an hour or two late. By mid-afternoon we were still waiting and by now becoming a little anxious as there was still a good way for us to travel. Another series of phone calls led us to believe that no vehicle could be expected at all so it would have to be a taxi, and the choice was very limited. Few if any appeared roadworthy and the one we chose proved the point. The luggage was thrown up onto the roof rack and I feared we should leave a trail of suitcases and rucksacks along every mile we covered. The passenger door would not close properly which necessitated a steadying hand at all times and to add to the difficulties, the window, when lowered, promptly fell completely out. The suspension felt nonexistent as we lurched our way from bump to bump, but ignorance is bliss and we had no wish to investigate further.

Some ten years earlier the system of main roads must have been quite reasonable, but through lack of funds little maintenance had been carried out since that time so that it was often better to drive along the shale hard-shoulder than risk the enormous potholes in the tarmac. It felt as if we were an entry in the African Safari Rally but actual speeds were difficult to assess as all the dials, including the speedometer and fuel gauge, just ticked irregularly like crazy metronomes.

Settling down to an acceptance of the situation, and having gained some familiarity with the road through the rust holes in the floor, we were brought up with a sudden thud which caused the collapse of the rear seat and an almighty hiss which was accompanied by the familiar flop of flat rubber against the road surface. Inconvenient, yes; bur prior to starting out we had taken care to note that there was a spare tyre on the roof rack. The jack was easily installed and the flat tyre removed and the other one was lowered down from the roof. Then the fun began as we discovered that the spare was also flat. We were stranded in an area that contrasted quite sharply with that previously described. The red soil had given way to a black powder and volcanic mounds, dominated by Mount Meru, were the main features of the landscape. The lack of rains had brought about the loss of many acres of newly planted woodland and the total failure of the maize crop.

The chill evening breeze gathered the fine dust into small whirlwind-like spinning tops which played to and fro around us. The road on one side was lined with giant sanseviera whose huge serrated leaves of green and yellow stripes, now coated with grey soot, at least gave us a little shelter from the all pervading grime. This was then our plight and our introduction to this alien continent and was also to be the first breakdown of many as cars and trucks were punished to the limit in these rough and dusty conditions. The saga slowly became more and more involved but eventually, by late that evening, we arrived in Arusha and made contact with Brother Adam and the rest of the party. They had merely run out of petrol on their way from the airport, an occurrence which appeared to be the norm in this country, and were now safely ensconced in the comfortable surroundings of the hotel.

The first day was spent at the Bee Research Department of the Serengeti Wildlife Institute with the Director, Liana Hassan, who accompanied us on all our further travels in Tanzania. He was a great help and made contact with the local beekeepers and arranged for us to enter forestry areas. together with the services of guides and an armed escort.

The majority of bees in Tanzania are kept in hollowed out cedar-log hives about 4 or 5ft (1.2 or 1.5m) in length and 15in (38cm) in diameter. These are cut lengthwise so that they divide into two-third and one-third portions. These two sections are then tightly secured at each end with metal bands and in this area of Mount Meru are suspended some 20ft (6m) up in the trees to prevent disturbance by insects such as the hive beetle or wood ants. At this height there is also a greatly reduced risk of theft and damage by the brush fires that occur from time to time. Most of the beekeepers in these forest areas belong to a co-operative consisting of about 20 members owning in total 500 or so of these log hives, each of which is branded with the name of the group. The hives are often as far as 25m (40km) from the home village so that expeditions into the hills lasting several days to collect the honey are quite routine.

First of all the smokers are lit some distance away from the log hives as the smell of smoke might easily provoke an attack from the bees before all is ready. A small hollow is made in the ground and in it a fire of elephant dung, which has been collected from the nearby paths, is made. Herbs are added and a lump of this smouldering excrement is transferred to the smoker. The native beekeepers believe that this ritual brings prosperity to the colonies and will curse the children of anyone who attempts to steal the honey. The hives were laboriously lowered by rope and then quietly opened, In the higher altitudes to the west of Kilimanjaro the hives are not placed so far from the ground, and are wedged in branches at about 10 or 15ft (3 or 4m), they can often be brought down by hand. The wild honeycomb was then carefully cut out and placed in a buffalo hide satchel. Not all the hives were occupied as it was just luck whether a swarm had entered it or not. A good colony produces on average 4 gal (20 litres) of crude honey each year from a mixed wild flora, which is then sold through the co-operative.

Roads were non existent in these areas so that the many miles covered along tracks worn by elephant and buffalo through dense woodland and at an altitude of 8,000 ft (2,438m) quite exhausted the team from Europe. Brother Adam himself after one such hike found it all too much, and on subsequent days he sent the remainder of the party to carry out the work of examining and assessing colonies and obtaining breeding stock as required. Actual beekeeping time was limited as we had a 2-hour drive followed by a 2-hour trek each day before we reached the vicinity of the hives and we could only journey safely during the hours of daylight because of the road conditions and also the danger from wild animals in the forest. Each evening, on our return, the group would report all their progress and experiences.

A day was also spent at one of the few commercial apiaries which in this instance was situated in the hot lowlands. The methods of beekeeping seemed extremely primitive and basic to us but such management techniques are in the main a direct result of the behaviour patterns of the yellow *Apis mellifera scutellata* bee that is indigenous to the area. Small nucleus 'bait' hives are situated in a mango orchard and when once a hive is occupied by a swarm, the bees are then transferred to a full-sized Langstroth hive in the main apiary. These colonies are checked at 10-day intervals for swarm cells, which are swiftly destroyed, but no other manipulations are attempted. One has to remember that this bee is very prone to swarming and absconding and also tends to fly off the combs making normal manipulations difficult. It is also both aggressive and unpredictable so that not only are the local people advised to stay indoors for several hours whilst the bees are being worked by flying a red flag, but medical supplies are also kept standing by should anyone be severely stung. The colonies are examined in the cool of the day, either early or late, as at these times when the bees are flying they seem less defensive.

Adam examined one unimpressive colony in the main apiary and whilst working the hive received just a few stings. However the onlookers, particularly the camera crew, were engulfed in a mass of raging yellow fighters that had been alerted from all the other hives in the apiary in spite of the fact that they had not been in the least disturbed. As Adam retreated the bees showed their true character, and had not returned to their hives but were still ready to attack an hour and a half later even in the vicinity of the house which was 1/4 mile (.4km) away. As he left the apiary Adam muttered, 'Just terrible, I have never known any other race of bee attack en masse as one body when only one small colony was disturbed'.

Honey is normally sold as a crude mixture of honey and wax as the wild combs are simply cut out and mashed up together. There are so few movable frame hives in the region that there is little need for centrifugal extractors. It was here, however, in the plains that we saw the only one in the whole vast area of Arusha district. It was a small four-frame hand-operated extractor which was in constant use each night. A few super combs were removed from each colony during the cool of the evening, extracted overnight, and replaced on the colonies the next morning. Such management systems could be vastly improved, and perhaps as funds become available for equipment more advanced techniques will gradually develop.

Expectations for the African trip had been extremely high, perhaps more so than on any other that Adam had undertaken, but it was not to be. It had begun badly on the day that he arrived, with Adam slipping and cutting his head severely which had necessitated a visit to the local hospital. Some what shaken by this he was determined to continue, but the heat and the altitude sapped every ounce of his energy. The results too were disappointing. Fewer hives than expected were examined and of those observed only one showed a pure uniform progeny. These bees, however, appeared very dark brown rather than coal black as described by earlier investigators, all the other colonies showing variations of colour to one degree or another, which pointed to a genetic mixture rather than a pure strain. The allotted time for the investigations was also very limited as Brother Adam had to cut short his trip as he was committed to attend Uppsala University in Sweden where he was to be awarded an honorary doctorate in praise of his service to beekeeping.

The final disaster was that all the caged queens that had been selected for breeding material were all dead by the time they arrived at Buckfast one week later. However the journey had been extremely informative and very much indicated a need for a complete survey of the honeybee population of Mount Kilimanjaro at regular altitude levels to determine both the migration patterns and the extent of cross-breeding between the black and yellow races. It appeared that, in the main, the higher altitudes were inhabited by the large dark bees which exhibited a quieter nature, whereas the lowlands supported the more aggressive yellow-orange banded *Apis mellifera scutellata*. In times of dearth, however, through periods of drought or high temperatures, the yellow bees would migrate up the slopes to higher, cooler regions whilst in times of plenty after the rains the reverse would happen. The two strains seem to interbreed quite happily so that a so-called hybrid barrier of great variation existed between the two extremes. However Brother Adam felt it was unlikely that a pure black bee, totally isolated from its yellow neighbours would be found even with further investigation. Time only allowed Adam one day in Kenya as the guest of Dr Kigatira, head of beekeeping in Nairobi, but this short visit reaffirmed his views that the pure black *monticola* bee, in an isolated situation, was unlikely to be found. However Adam is hopeful that he will be able to obtain useful breeding stock from the area of Mount Kenya in the future.

Needless to say the ceremonies in Sweden that had abruptly ended the Africa trip were most overwhelming and completely faded any disappointment Brother Adam may have felt for any lost days of the previous week. Adam's supporters gathered to witness the regal events with pride and delight as their old friend accepted the ring and tall black hat of a Doctor of Science. Lavish parties and celebrations followed and Brother Adam was still elated when he returned to sleepy Devon three days later, laden with the Swedish newspapers which had given his award full coverage. Perhaps it is a little ironic that the pinnacle of his achievements is the recognition of his work by the very establishments that Brother Adam has so long felt followed rather academic paths that had no practical application for the commercial beekeeper.

Chapter 13
Brother Adam, The Final Chapter

Inevitably as the years pass our abilities fail and though exceptional for a nonagenarian Brother Adam was finding the daily tasks arduous. He had suffered with his eyes for some years in the form of glaucoma and I had often taken him to London for his six monthly visits to his ophthalmologist in Harley Street. Cataract had complicated the problem and Adam decided that he would take up the offer of the French bee-keepers to pay for the eye operation to be done by a leading surgeon in France. This was a great success, although he was still worried about his sight. His hearing and balance was becoming increasingly difficult through Menieres disease. In fact on one occasion he had fallen in the car park and knocked himself unconcious to be found like a wet rag lying in the pouring rain some time later, by Father Leo. Although he had a strong supporting team in the form of Peter Donovan and Brother Daniel his hopes of finding a super bee-keeper amongst the bretheren was a wishful one. Who could possibly replace him? His standards were fixed and very high and his methods were uncompromising.

There had been recurring problems with the production of queen bees for U.K. sales. It had always been Brother Adam's firm belief that the breeding and evaluation of queens should be executed under his watchful eye in the difficult climate at Buckfast. However the high annual rainfall in summer in recent years and unpredictability of the weather was not conducinve to the commercial rearing of queens. Thus selected breeding stock had been sent to various commercial establishments. The onset of varroasis in Europe and other various bee diseases had meant many and varied restrictions on bee imports. Various projects had been tried and had proved quite unsatisfactory and Brother Adam found the task of orgnizing such programmes very onerous at his age. The Buckfast Queens that had been offered for sale in the U.K at that time, were inconsistent. The colour had been very dark in some cases and the temperament disappointing. This of course brought its own problems of dissatisfied customers. As Adam himself had completed some of the contracts without any advice from the legal department, the Abbey had been presented with the odd legal tangle. Times at the Abbey had changed, in that Father David Charlesworth had been elected as Abbot, replacing Adam's longtime friend Dom. Leo Smith. New brooms sweep clean and Father David wanted all the community to observe closely the rule of St. Benedict. Adam had often voiced the opinion that there were elements in the Abbey that did not enjoy his fame and the honours and gifts that had been bestowed on him. After all, first and foremost he was a Benedictine monk. In the spring of 1992, it was decided that Brother Adam should retire from the rigours of the bee department and continue to enjoy the discussions and correspondance with eminent bee-keepers, especially those abroad.

Father Leo would take on the role as figure head of the department, and host the many visiting bee-keepers and deal with all the correspondance. Peter Donovan and Brother Daniel, with occasional help from Brother Laurence would carry on the beekeeping work with a greater accent on honey production which had been dissapointingly poor, in recent years. Brother Adam vehemently disagreed and wanted to engage an eminent European beekeeper to run the department for a minimum of five years. This was totally against Abbey policy as one of the community always took position of head of department although they did employ a number of ancilliary staff. The Abbot was not for turning. Adam misunderstood completley the reasoning behind the decision and the idea that he had been ousted after all these years of service was firmly fixed in his head. He set about rallying the troops and wrote to his contacts in the media and to his friends abroad. Unfortunately today fame brings speculation and controversy and such topics are hot stuff in the national newspapers as well as local press. I visited the Abbot to try to diffuse the situation but the damage had been done. Adam had set the hare running and it was best to let it complete its course. Naturally the Abbott was dismayed at the whole saga and although he agreed to see me his attitude was cold and matter of fact. I recieved letters from far and wide but I felt a non-commital reply stating that I was constantly in touch with Adam would best serve him. With time I felt the problems would resolve and Adam would realize that everyone had his best interests at heart, including the Abbot.

Adam felt that his position was untenable so he decided to visit his cousin in Germany and think things through. He returned in the Autumn before the winter set in. As the months passed it became clear that Adam needed more care. He had retained his room opposite the honey house which had been very conveient for his work and his many visitors like me who wanted to drop in and see him without an official visit. It also meant that he could bang away on his type-writer from four in the early hours of the morning without disturbing anyone. However this room was some away from the other cells and not at all convenient for anyone who wished to keep an eye on him as he suffered one or two blackouts or provide nursing care. But Adam was determined not to move. In the spring he decided that he would go north for a holiday and stay with his friends in Northumberland. Unfortunately while he was away he became ill and this neccessitated a visit to Durham hospital and then he was transferred to Ashburn hospital, near Buckfast. Regrettably it was therefore decided that he would be best in a nearby residential home. The transition was difficult. He had lived at the St. Mary's Abbey for over eighty years and the regime of early to bed and very early starts was not one that fitted in with the home. He became confused and at times felt persecuted. I visited him often and he always enjoyed the flowers of the season-primroses, daffodils, honeysuckle and of course heather. All things that reminded him of Dartmoor that he loved so much. Time heals and it was not long before a picture of Adam celebrating his ninety-sixth birthday appeared in the local press and he seemed to have settled. The old stories and the tales of his travels and his bees never failed to arouse a chuckle.

As the hills turned purple with the blooming of the heather in the September of that year, 1996 Adam ceased his fight.

As a monk, Brother Adam had, as already mentioned, lived a priveleged life following his love of bees, without the encumbrances of everyday life, of bills and taxes and family problems. He felt he had served his God through his bees and had given his life to them. His unique situation had enabled him to bring a dedication and singleness of purpose to commercial beekeeping that is unparalleled in modern apiculture. In the words of `Professor Frederich Ruttner: " Brother Adam's life long work has contributed substantially to the improvement of management and stocks of bees. This contribution to apicultural research, which in turn has had its impact on honeybee breeding has yet to be fully recognized. "

Bibliography

Galthorne-Hardy, Jonathon,
Inside the Cloister
(Buckfast Abbey, 1984)

Herrod-Hempsall, W.,
Bee-keeping New and Old Described with Pen and Camera, 2 vols
(The *British Bee Journal*, 1930)

Prince, Elizabeth,
Dartmoor Seasons
(Devon Books, 1987)

Wedmore, E. B.,
A Manual of Beekeeping
(Edward Arnold & Co, 1932: 2nd ed 1945)

Articles

Anderson, John, 'A Great-Name-F. W. L. Sladen',
Bee World Vol III No 5
(October 1921)

Carlisle, Elizabeth,
'Biometrical Investigations of some European and other Races of Honey Bees',
Bee World, 36 no 3
(March 1955)

Malden, W., 'A Report on the progression of the Isle of Wight Disease',
British Beekeeping Journal, XXXIX
(1911)

Oertel, E., 'The Mating Flights of Queen Bees',
Gleanings in Bee Culture, 68
(1940), 292-3, 333

Rennie, J., White, P. B. and Harvey. E. J., 'The Isle of Wight Disease in Hive Bees',
Transactions of the Royal Society, LII, Part IV, no 29
(1919)

Ruttner, F., 'The Mating of the Honeybee;, *Bee World*, 37 no 1
(January 1956)

Ruttner, F.,
'The Cretan Bee' *Apidologie*, 11 1104
(1980)

Ruttner, F. and Mackensen, O., 'The Genetics of the Honeybee',
Bee World, 33 no 4
(April 1952)

Sugden, M. A. and Furgula, B., 'The Evaluation of Six Commercial Honeybee Stocks used in Minnesota', *American Bee Journal*
(February 1982)

Transactions of the Tropical Beekeepers Congress (1974, 1985)

Books by Brother Adam
Bee-keeping in Buckfast Abbey (British Bee Publications Ltd, 1975) also available in French and German

In Search of the Best Strains of Bees, second edition (Northern Bee Books, 1983) also available in French, German and Swedish

Breeding the Honeybee (Northern Bee Books, 1987) also available in German

Chronology

1898   Born 3 August in the village of Mittel Biberach.
1910   18 March; arrives at Buckfast and enters the alumnate where he is known as Louis.
1914   Becomes a novitiate and labours as a stonemason on the building of the abbey.
1915   Because of ill health Adam joins Brother Columban with the bees. The Isle of Wight disease first reaches Devon.
1916   Is given the name Adam and is now able to wear the full habit of St Benedict.
1919   Adam takes over full responsibility for the bees. 1920 The first 'out apiary' is established at Staverton Bridge Farm and the writings of Professor Armbruster give him his first ideas on bee breeding.
1922   August; Adam takes his final vows.
1925   The isolation mating station at Sherberton on Dartmoor is established.
1929/30 The home apiary is resited and work commences on re-organisation of the honey department.
1932   Adam falls ill and returns home to Germany for the first time.
1939   A second visit to Germany is made as his mother is in poor health. He meets his cousin, Maria, for the first time, but in the winter his health breaks down and he is advised never to work again.
1947   He visits Germany again and later that year his mother dies.
1950   The first journeys begin; France - Switzerland - Austria - Italy - Sicily - Germany.
1952   North Africa - Algeria - Israel - Jordan Syria - Lebanon - Cyprus - Greece – Yugoslavia Ligurian Alps.
1954   Greece, Asia Minor and the Aegean islands. 1956 Western Yugoslavia and the Aegean.1959 Iberian Peninsula, Spain and Portugal. 1962 Morocco, Southern Turkey and Egypt. 1972 Turkey. 1974 OBE is awarded to Brother Adam for services to bee keeping.
1975   Verdienstkreuz is awarded in Germany. 1976 Greece, Slovenia, Morocco.
1977   Greece.
1980   The Cretan bee is named *Apis mellifera* adami.
1981   Visit to the Isle of Athos.
1987   Expedition to East Africa and then to Uppsala University in Sweden to receive an Honorary DsC from the Faculty of Agriculture.
1989   Honorary doctorate, Exeter University 1993 Retires from beekeeping Department. 1994 Moves to nursing home. 1996 1st September, Died.

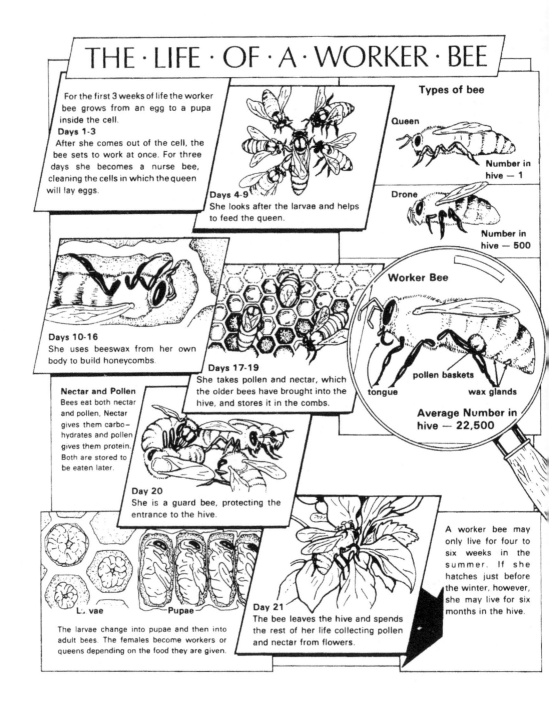

FROM · FLOWER · TO · JAR

Where the honey comes from.

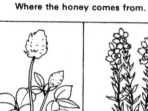

Clover   Heather

In spring the bees collect nectar from clover. In the summer the beekeeper takes them to Dartmoor to gather nectar from the heather.

How to collect honey without getting stung.

The beekeeper wears gloves and a hat with a veil, for protection. He is sometimes stung, though.

The beekeeper uses smoke to make the bees think their hive is on fire. They try to save the honey by eating it and this makes them sleepy, so they leave the beekeeper alone.

Taking the honey from the comb.

Hot Knife

With a hot knife the beekeeper takes the caps off the honey cells. The combs are put into the honey extractor, which is a machine like a spin dryer.

As the extractor spins round, the honey is thrown on to the sides of the drum. Then it is put into jars.

A warm humid summer is needed for a lot of honey to be made. In the last 15 years less honey has been produced because the summers have been too wet, or too dry.

Winter Work.

Every winter the beekeeper cleans the hives. He sterilises them, repaints them and replaces old combs with new ones.

Lightning Source UK Ltd.
Milton Keynes UK
UKHW030700250820
368797UK00009B/1952